Colby and Me

Colby and Me

H. L. Wegley

Order this book online at www.trafford.com
or email orders@trafford.com

Most Trafford titles are also available at major online book retailers.

Printed in Victoria, BC, Canada.

ISBN: 978-1-4269-1818-6 (soft)
ISBN: 978-1-4269-1819-3 (hard)

Library of Congress Control Number: 2009938785

*Our mission is to efficiently provide the world's finest, most comprehensive book publishing
service, enabling every author to experience success. To find out how to publish your
book, your way, and have it available worldwide, visit us online at www.trafford.com*

Trafford rev. 11/4/2009

 www.trafford.com

North America & international
toll-free: 1 888 232 4444 (USA & Canada)
phone: 250 383 6864 ♦ fax: 812 355 4082

To Colby

Andrew Gold's song title pretty much says it all, "Thank You for Being a Friend."

Acknowledgments

Colby—you're the friend that made my childhood worth living. I can't imagine how dull it would have been and how little I would have learned about life, fun, and living on the edge (something we all need to do at times) if I hadn't known you. Best wishes to you, my friend, as we enter the golden years of our lives. On the flip side, you got a little payback from your own son, didn't you?

Babe—thanks for the countless hours of reading, listening to, re-reading and re-listening to these stories to help me get them down for others to enjoy. But mostly, thanks for the forty th—uh, well, all of those post-Colby-and-me years that you have given me. Many have been as breathless as our diving suit (but in a much, much better way).

Dan and Dennis R—though I only got to run with you guys for two or three years, you were two great guys for any boy to know. Not only were you good friends, but you were the dream friends for any teenage boy. I think your Dad had every tool known to man and we used most of them. I still think about your little sister, Dilly, every time I hear that oldie song, "Lavender Blue." I think Colby really liked her, but he wouldn't admit it at the time. "Lavender blue, Dilly, Dilly…"—nobody sang it like Sammy Turner, 1959—it hit #3 on the charts!

Ronnie K—sure wish you hadn't killed Pal. I mean, sorry you got your leg broken when Pal ran under the front wheel of your motorcycle. Pal was just a biscuit-eating bloodhound, but we loved him. He could sure run! His speed was probably his undoing—a little slower and he never would have caught up with your bike and, well, more biscuits would have been wolfed down. By the way, did arthritis eventually set in in your leg? Bet it did! If you went into meteorology like I did, and had an injury like you had, your forecasting accuracy would go up several percentage points about the time you hit 55.

Larry R—did you end up going to OSU like your big brother? What did you really think when you saw Colby's face after he "blew it clear off?" Sure loved our fishing trip to Baby Foot Lake! Chumming's a great way to catch trout, isn't it?

Don B—did you ever tell Ann about you and Gerd roaring through the halls of old GPHS on your Honda? Bet you didn't! How goes the fishing up in Alaska?

Vaughn B—I've never known anyone who could turn into silly putty and ooze out of an opponents grasp like you could. That sure came in handy when you were wrestling, didn't it? Does your boy still talk about him killing the grizzly that was breaking into your cabin when he was ten? I'll bet he does. Did you move to Alaska too?

Wayne W—thanks for all those shots you sank from the corner. When I was at the point and couldn't make anything happen because the defense was swarming everywhere, I could always look for you on the right corner. Got a question for you—ran over any cows lately?

Jerry D—I still miss you after all of these years, good buddy. We had a lot in common. I sure hope that you are in a much better place and that you're there to welcome me through the gates some day. We have to put our trust in other drivers to some degree each time we pull out onto a highway. Sometimes that trust isn't warranted, as you found out so many years ago.

Frank M—I lost track of you after high school. One good thing about that contest with the static generator is that the hairdo it gave you was right in style about seven years later. After the charge you took, I'd bet you still had that hairdo seven years later!

Mike B—I heard you're back in the southern Oregon area now. You're one of the lucky ones down there in the warm, sunny Rogue River Valley while I'm up here in Seattle looking at gray and hoping for blue.

Gil M—man where'd you go after the ninth grade? Either you dropped of the face of the earth or maybe those electrodes you hung on to did more damage than we thought.

Mr. Ford—thanks for turning me on to science. But what I really liked was when you refereed the Medford basketball games. You just kept blowing the whistle and we kept winning. You must really hate that nasty Black Tornado!

Howard P—you were a real example of a man who appreciates humor. Maybe that compliment will get me off the hook for using your motorcycle ride as an example of enhanced oxidation.

Danny—sure hope things came together for the better for you. Hope the time we spent together helped point you toward clean fun, even if it was a bit dangerous. By the way, did you ever spot Elly May?

Orie—since I couldn't find you to get permission, I changed your name. If perchance you read this book, thanks for showing Colby and me not only the trucker's knot, but an example of a young man who is committed to his family even through very hard times—one who was humble enough to work at whatever was available to meet his family's needs. There aren't enough like you these days.

Colby's Uncle John and Aunt Ethel—thanks for the impact you had on our lives and for the stories you told us about your Wild West days in Texas.

Colby's Mom and Dad—thanks for allowing me to spend all that time at your house when I was growing up and thanks also for all those years of being second parents to me.

Mom and Dad—thanks for letting me spend all that time with Colby. Dad, I know how you loved humor—I hope that somehow you get a chance to read this book as you're walking those golden streets— I think you'd like it.

Grandpa T—thanks for all you taught me about hunting and fishing, even if the fishing part made my mouth sore.

Cheryl O—you are one of those who also disappeared after high school. Hope it wasn't due to the stigma of me leaking that you were going out with an underclassman.

Steve N—hope you don't mind that I told your secret about Cheryl—guys don't usually mind such things being revealed. Also, thanks for helping to bring home that state championship trophy in football!

Maria—hope you don't mind being cast as a young public defender in this book. You would have been pretty good too if you just wouldn't have drawn that hanging judge every time you went to court.

Dale W and Jon W—I heard you're both retired and are living in the Grants Pass area. We'll have to get together some time when I'm down there—that is, if you don't hold it against me that I rolled that refrigerator-sized rock down on you guys.

Ronald—as you grow older and that memory thing starts affecting you, try not to forget this—don't play with kitties that have a white stripe down their back!

Colby's Uncle Garth—hope they let you fly in through those pearly gates! I also hope they let you video the whole thing!

AJ—sorry for hiding all of your jewelry and sending you on a treasure hunt all over the woods to get it back. It sounded like a good idea at the time to Colby and me. I still haven't forgiven you for making Colby and me walk down Cemetery Road at 1 AM after watching <u>UFO</u> (grin).

Dr. Robson—I'm still amazed at how quickly you ended my poison oak misery. Maybe sometime after we all meet together in the air I can hear about your missionary trips to India.

Dr. Johnson—thanks for all of the house calls you made when I should have been in the hospital but we couldn't afford it. Sorry I turned down your offer of a scholarship to medical school. That is one of those things that, looking back, I wish I could change.

Mr. Dickinson—thanks for all you taught me. Much of what I learned about playing football and running track I learned from you—especially since you coached me for almost 4 years—4 years that I had to endure the nickname you stuck me with, Wig. "Wig, run 23 crossfire on 5 and tell them nobody jumps offside!" Remember?

Buddy M—thanks for organizing all of those neighborhood cowboy and Indian wars. Heard you moved to Idaho. Bet you're retired by now—I hope so.

Thanks to the team at Trafford Publishing for your help in getting these stories about Colby and me printed, bound and distributed. You all were great!

Table of Contents

Prologue

Colby and I grew up in the best place in the best country at the very best time ever to be kids. You can't beat the good ol' USA—everybody wants in and nobody wants out (unlike most other countries).

By the time Colby and I were born we had antibiotics. Without them I wouldn't have lived long enough for our friendship to occur. About the time we really became aware of Polio, we had the Salk vaccine. From the time we were cognizant of wars, we had only the cold war to worry about. But, we knew our beloved Ike would take care of us. Worst case, if somebody pressed the button, we knew there was nothing in southern Oregon that the USSR would want to bomb. Also we were told that the upper air flow in the northern hemisphere nearly always shielded us from any serious fallout from nuclear blasts.

It was not until we were adults that we had to deal with war. Colby and I both became Viet Nam era vets. But let's get back to the good stuff—Colby and I lived in southern Oregon, a virtual paradise for young boys. Besides the Pacific Ocean, the many rivers, and hundreds of lakes, we had millions and millions of acres of uninhabited forest land to wander as far as our legs could carry us in a day without even seeing signs of civilization. To top it all off, we had four distinct seasons with summers long and warm enough to give us the maximum time to enjoy the outdoors.

We were raised before those doggoned no-fault divorce laws brought the marriage meltdown. Only one kid in my whole school came from a family that had experienced a divorce. No kid I knew ever worried about being snatched by some maniac while playing, while out in public, or anywhere for that matter. There were no drugs in southern Oregon—they came later when the hippies invaded us after leaving San Francisco.

We had no real worries as kids except report cards or, as we grew older, zits. All in all, it was a time for just enjoying being a kid without anyone or anything trying to speed up our growing up process. To top all of that off, I had a best friend, Colby, who when combined with all of those other "bests" gave me the best childhood of any kid that ever lived—at least I think so.

As I said, my best friend was Colby. Now, we didn't go around telling everybody we were best friends (you know, like girls do). We didn't even tell each other. Heck, we didn't need to. The things we did together demonstrated our relationship better than words ever could describe it.

Those things that we did, at least the ones I'm willing to put down in black and white, are what this book is all about. I think you'll see that Colby and I had more fun together than any two boys ought to have. If our parents knew even half of what we did, they definitely would agree.

You must keep in mind that, though we did some risky things, our parents were not negligent parents. They cared a lot about us. But, because of our two dads being like they were, we got to do a lot of stuff that most boys can only dream of. Here's how that came about. You see, my Dad was a born worrier. By the time I was four or five I had that figured out. I also calculated that his paranoia was going to severely limit what I got to do. Dad's philosophy was, "The less a kid gets to do, the safer he is." And, Dad wanted me to be really safe.

Colby's Dad, on the other hand, had a much different philosophy of child rearing. He thought that you ought to teach your kids what is right and what is wrong and then you just trust that if they were meant to live to a ripe old age, the Lord would see to it that they did. So Colby got to do a lot of fun stuff—stuff that I wanted to be a part of.

By the time I was six, Colby and I had become best friends and so were our parents. I don't mean to brag, but I was a pretty shrewd observer of adult behavior even as a youngster. At about this time, I perceived that no grown man wants to admit to another grown man that he's a worrier. As John Wayne would say, "It's a sign of weakness." It took only a short time for me to learn that, as long as I could keep my Dad around Colby's Dad, when Colby got permission to do something, my Dad wasn't' about to tell me I couldn't do it too. That would have been "a sign of weakness."

We knew we had my Dad over a barrel, but we weren't about let him know what we knew. That would have spoiled our fun.

If you're a kid that doesn't get to do much, my advice to you is to find a friend who's got a Dad like Colby's and try to get your Dads to visit or do things together. When the two Dads are together, well, that's when you pop the question (whatever the question of the day happens to be).

Another thing you need to know before reading this book is that the stories in it are true—that is, they describe events that really happened. We live in a postmodern society where truth is in question and therefore all of history along with it. Words are painted as being conveyors of, well, not much at all. But, because you're reading these words, I know you really don't believe all that fashionable nonsense. You know that words mean a great deal and let me assure you the words that you are reading are history as lived by Colby and me—at least they are history best as I can remember it in my mind, in my imagination, and in my heart.

Now, I kept my own name in these stories (I, me), but my buddy's name was tweaked a bit to protect him. While I have confessed most of the sins and follies of my youth to my parents and to others and have been forgiven (for the most part)—I'm not so sure about Colby. Therefore, I did tweak his name somewhat. If he reads this book (sure hope he doesn't), he will know immediately what I mean by "tweaked." For the uninitiated, that remains a mystery that, if you are so inclined, you can solve as you read this book, search the internet, or use any other resources at your disposal.

You may notice that the vocabulary changes a bit from story to story. That's because I told the stories like I remembered them, using my vocabulary at the time the story was imprinted on the static RAM of my mind (lately I'm finding my RAM isn't as static as it once was). Since the stories are not in chronological order, you may hear an eight-year old talking in one story, then a tween or a teen in the next. Just go with the flow!

One final thing for the benefit of any youngsters reading this book—swear to me right now that you won't try to imitate any of the things that Colby and I tried. None of them! Swear it! Because, if you copy us, you are sure to blow yourselves up, burn yourselves up, die of poisoning, drown, fall to your death, smother, get shot, get arrested, or some combination of these things.

Please understand that Colby and I lived in gentler times. Half a century ago, we had much more land to roam. The land was occupied by far fewer people and it was a land where there were far fewer really bad people and far fewer bad things happened. So, somehow, we survived. You won't!

But, if you do have the urge to grow up dangerously, instead of living out that urge, I urge you instead to live it vicariously through these stories about Colby and me.

The Church Chapters

For Colby and me, much of our young lives involved, and were shaped by, events that took place in that little country church house where Colby's Great Uncle John preached for many years. This church had its origin in the early 1800's in what has been called the Restoration Movement. As such, the church had a set of doctrinal distinctives that provided a rich source to draw upon for the stories about Colby and me.

I can still see Uncle John preaching using a magnifying glass to see his Bible after his eyes grew weak. The magnifying glass gave those in the pews fleeting glimpses of a huge nose, then an enormous eye, or a cavernous mouth. Just when the magnified facial features were about to make me laugh, Uncle John would pound his point home with authority as he stepped away from the podium and whopped the little oil stove with his thick King James Bible causing it to ring for 20 or 30 seconds while he let his point sink in.

Well, Colby and I learned a lot of things and, as you are about to read (in the next three stories), tried to learn even more during those church services. We got into mischief always, and into trouble sometimes, as Colby and I wrote that part of our lives that I have called, "The Church Chapters."

1
The Church Without
A Sunday School

On just about any given Sunday, if you walked into our little country church house, you would see Colby and me sitting together in the front row of seats. I say seats because our church house didn't have plain old pews. We had theater seats! They were old, made of iron and wood, but nevertheless, they were seats, not pews.

Pews weren't the only thing we didn't have at our church. We didn't have Sunday school. But that was because of a certain view of the scriptures taken by our elders. Now we believed in all the basic Christian stuff like: Jesus was born of the virgin Mary; He never did anything wrong; He was crucified and died; after three days "Up from the Grave He Arose" (that was a song in our hymnal); and we believed in the atonement.

Atonement is just a big word that means something like this: All of us do some bad stuff when we are alive and we pay for that by dying. But, our dying is worth just barely enough to pay for all the bad stuff we did. So, when we die, we don't have anything left over to give to St. Peter to pay our way through the Pearly

Gates and into heaven. But, Jesus didn't do anything bad. Even when he was a little boy, he didn't hang grasshoppers, steal old dynamite to blow up old cars, or get into trouble in church—he didn't do any of that stuff. So he didn't have to pay for anything when he died. That means he has enough left to leave at the Pearly Gates to pay anyone's way into heaven if they really want him to.

Now if your pastor or Sunday school teacher uses that word, atonement, you can raise your hand and say, "I know what atonement means." But if your teacher, or anybody else asks you what it means, you gotta' tell it right—like I just told you. OK?

As I was saying, our church had a few unusual things that it believed in. But rather than believe in stuff, mostly we just didn't believe in stuff. We didn't believe in using musical instruments; we didn't believe in using a bunch of communion cups or more than one loaf of communion bread; we didn't believe in paying our preacher, we didn't believe in missing church unless you were really sick, and we didn't believe in Sunday school.

Some of you probably had really great Sunday school teachers that told you all of those Old Testament stories like Noah and the ark—when all those people laughed at Noah for building the ark but, when the water started coming and they wanted in, then God shut the door and they all drowned. Naaman—remember him— he was the soldier that got leprosy and then got cured from leprosy by dipping in muddy water. I'll bet some of you even got to see stories like those in colored flannelgraphs.

Well, Colby and I felt cheated. Because of our parents' beliefs, we missed out on all those stories. Even worse, another thing our church didn't believe in was preaching from the Old Testament. We just went through the New Testament one chapter a week, starting in Matthew 1. It didn't matter whether the chapter was ten verses or sixty verses long. Sometimes we got out early and sometimes the sermon lasted forever. But, when we got through Revelation 22, it was just "First and ten, do it again, we like it, we like it" So, we didn't even get to hear those good old stories in a sermon.

As I said, we felt cheated and we decided to do something about it. You see, there was this herkin' big King James Bible that lay in the front of the church, mostly because it looked good there. Colby and I asked his Dad (who was one of the elders) if we could read that Bible during the sermon. As long as we were quiet, he didn't care at all if we read it. But we found out that in order to read it, we had to be sure we got it before the service started.

The first time we sat down with that big Bible, Colby set it on his lap and, when the sermon started, opened the front part over into my lap. It filled both of our laps and a little bit more. Now don't be thinking that herkin' big King James Bible was just any old Bible because it wasn't. It had full page pictures for all the main stories. It had the biggest concordance I have ever seen. It also had, what I called, the Sunday school page. This page contained an index of story titles. It even told where to find the story in the Bible. The story titles there would take any boy's mind and imagination and suck them in like a vacuum cleaner. There were titles like, "Man Gets Swallowed by a Whale", or "Woman Drives a Nail through a Man's Head" (that was one of my favorites), or "The Donkey that Talked."

Well we'd never read anything like that in our Bibles, or anywhere else for that matter, so while the preacher preached, Colby and I had our own little Sunday school class each week. The way we would pick a story was that one of us would run our finger down the index, line-by-line. At each entry the other one of us would shake their head yes or no. If the answer was yes, we flipped the herkin' big King James Bible to the scripture reference and began to read silently together.

Gradually we began to learn about the Old Testament, which we liked. Also, we were quiet in church, which our moms and dads liked.

All went well until that Sunday when Colby found that passage in 1st Kings. I still can't remember for sure how he found it. It wasn't listed in the index of stories. Oh, I remember now. Colby was looking in the exhaustive concordance in the back of the Bible to see if God ever used any bad words. I think he figured if God ever used bad words then it let Colby off the hook for the times he used them.

You see, Colby found a pretty interesting word that was used in 1st Kings 16:11. We backed up a few verses before that point and started to read—you know, you're supposed to do that to get the context right. We read about this soldier, Zimri, who was a traitor so he started killing people. When he came to Baasha's family, it says that Zimri killed them so they couldn't pee on the wall anymore (I think it must be just referring to the men).

Well that part about peeing on the wall right there in God's word struck me as being funny—so funny that I tried not to laugh. But, the harder I tried, the bigger the laugh inside of me seemed to grow and the more it tried to come out. Just as the preacher got real quiet to let the effect of his point sink in, I snickered. There was so much pressure behind that snicker that it just came—well, it came asnickering out—really loud!

Immediately every head in the building turned up and then turned toward me. I lowered my head and turned it toward the Bible. But, when I looked at the Bible, there was that "peeing on the wall" phrase and I snickered again. One of the heads that turned and the attached body started moving toward me. I looked up and, in horror, saw that it was my Dad. He grabbed me by the shoulder very firmly. I was led in great embarrassment, shame and utter humiliation to a seat beside Dad and then once again our church became a church without a Sunday school.

If you ever decide to attend a church like ours, you must promise me this. When you tell your kids bed time stories, tell them those Old Testament Bible stories. Kids love to hear about Samson with his eyes poked out pushing over that big pillar and smashing all those Philistines. And Isaac just about getting stabbed by his Dad (I felt like Isaac that day). Please, you gotta' make sure you tell them about Zimri and the "peeing on the wall" because no little kid should have to suffer from snicker stifling after reading that one cold turkey in church.

If you're tempted to not tell your kids those stories, then at least tell them about Colby and me as a warning. Also you should consider if you really want to risk your kids embarrassing you in church when they rummage through their concordance looking for bad words, or their curiosity takes them into the Old Testament and they see the word the King James Bible uses for "donkey" used in some funny context (like when Balaam whipped his, uh, donkey) and it makes them snicker out loud? So, either make sure that you tell your kids those stories at home or just don't take them to a church without a Sunday school.

2
Pal Goes Forward

He was a shameless hound. He never admitted to anything wrong, except maybe to hunker with his tail tucked in and that was a rarity. He generally did whatever he wanted and what he wanted was determined by his current impulse. Colby and I still loved him, but as a kid I would have put money down that nobody could ever write a true story called, "Pal Goes Forward."

It was a blistering hot Sunday morning. Before the service was over, which was usually about 11:45AM, we would already be flirting with a triple-digit temperature. Because the little church house didn't have air conditioning (nobody we knew had it in those days), and because it didn't have any fans, Colby's folks would slip over to the church well before the service started and open all the windows down one side of the church, while propping the front door open, to keep things a little cooler in the building.

As a meteorologist with many years of research in atmospheric physics, I can now understand the micrometeorology behind the window and door configuration used by Colby's parents. They had minimized heating from solar radiation and also minimized advection of warm air into the building. They must have been pretty smart because Colby's folks knew how to do this without having a single college course in meteorology.

There was, however, a drawback to leaving the front door of the church wide open. You see, one of those other things we didn't believe in was having ushers. So nobody was watching for whoever or whatever might want to come in the front door.

At the time, Colby had only owned his blood hound, Pal, for about six months. But six months was more than enough time for the gangly, awkward, adolescent hound to really bond with Colby.

Pal always tracked whatever Pal wanted to track—he never did learn to be a true hunting dog. This morning Pal wanted to track Colby and so he put his cold, wet nose to the ground and sniffed out Colby's trail as far as the front door of the church. Now, this particular morning was Colby's Dad's turn to preach. The elders in our little church rotated that responsibility among themselves because, as you might remember, we didn't believe in having paid preachers.

As Colby's Dad's eyes rose from his Bible and focused on something at the back of the building where the front door was, from my place beside Colby I turned my head to follow our preacher's gaze. There I saw Pal standing in the doorway with his eyes locked on Colby, who was seated at the inside seat of the front row of the church.

Several possible scenarios ran through my mind like, Colby's Dad runs Pal out of the church amid barking and great commotion, or Colby's Dad tells Colby to remove his hound from the church causing Colby great embarrassment and damaging the boy-dog and boy-Dad relationships, or Pal comes bounding down the aisle to meet Colby while baying like he's out of his mind disrupting the entire service and is henceforth tied up during church services forever. Well, those scenarios were all wrong!

Pal, uncharacteristically quiet, began to walk the aisle of the church. That forced me to quickly revise my list of possible scenarios. But, I quickly became more interested in the one true scenario that was playing out, so I sat back and watched it. But, as I did, one stubborn little question kept tickling the backside of my mind, "How is Colby's Dad gonna handle a penitent Pal?"

You see whenever anyone walked the aisle at our church, sometimes called "going forward," it was usually because they were penitent about something—that is they needed to confess something and repent of it. But Pal was going forward during the sermon, well before the invitation (when people usually would go forward). So, a little while before we sang the invitation song, "Jesus Is Calling," Pal evidently felt Colby calling and he confidently and quietly walked the aisle right to the spot where a penitent person would walk to—right beside Colby, where Pal quietly sat down.

Now, I knew Pal really wasn't penitent because when he was really ashamed of something, he just tucked his tail between his legs and slunk away. That was the nearest thing to a confession of wrongdoing that you could ever get out of him.

When Pal first approached Colby I wanted to lean over and say, "Whatever you do, don't tell Pal to sit. He never minds and usually starts howling when you try to make him do anything he doesn't want to do." But I held off giving my advice and just sat there uneasily as did nearly everyone in the church building.

I smiled and relaxed when Colby just reached over and patted Pal's head—a surprising and most welcome development. At least Pal wouldn't start howling immediately.

But what really surprised me was how Colby's Dad handled the situation. He never missed a beat; he just kept on preaching calmly, as was his manner of speaking, and he allowed Pal to sit by his beloved master, Colby, thereby sparing Colby the embarrassment of having to remove his hound from church in the presence of the whole congregation. Until the service ended Pal just sat there basking in Colby's presence and enjoying those occasional pats on the head.

I can't remember if Colby's Dad was preaching on a passage about faith, Christian fellowship, or love or something else. Regardless, the object lesson he gave me by letting the boy and his dog share that moment together, taught me much more than whatever chapter he was expositorily teaching through could ever have taught.

I'll never know how Colby's Dad knew Pal wouldn't erupt into one of his baying, bounding fits, creating total chaos in our church service. Maybe there's a lot more to faith, wisdom, knowing what's right, and knowing what's best for your child than I knew at the time. Evidently so, because Colby's Dad surprised me when he demonstrated all of those things the morning that Pal went forward.

3
Stock Still In Church

In our little one-room country church house there was something that you saw virtually every warm Sunday morning—bees. They made for some interesting times during church services. But there was one thing you never saw in any Sunday service anytime of the year, which was Colby being stock still in church.

Our church had bees in its belfry! Now I don't mean that our people were mad as in looney, or mad as a hornet, or anything like that. We just had a permanent infestation of bees in the attic of the church house.

The bees went dormant in winter time, but on the first warm, sunny spring day, they were back. The warmer the day, the more bees you saw.

I should clarify here that our bees were those things some people called mud dobbers and other people call dirt dobbers. Regardless, they sure dobbed a lot of mud or dirt in the attic of our church. The first time Colby and I stuck our heads up through the little door in the ceiling and into the attic, I was amazed that the ceiling hadn't fallen in. I'm sure glad that churches are tax exempt— at least they were when Colby and I were kids. If we had to pay property tax, one look in the attic and the assessor would realize that we had half the land in the county up there. Heck, we could never have paid our taxes! If things keep going the way they are in our country, a lot of churches may have a hard time paying their taxes (but that's another story that probably doesn't belong in this book).

Now, if you attended our church, here is what you would see at a typical summer service. As you entered and took a seat in one of our theater seats, you might see one mud dobber flying around the ceiling.

This is how the mud dobbers flew—well, I wouldn't call it flying, because it was a combination of flying and falling. A bee would squeeze out of the hot attic and fly out. But I guess those bees just had so much lift in their wings when they flew that they always arced up until they hit the ceiling. The collision with the ceiling temporarily interfered with their wing motion, so the bee would fall; but, then it started flapping its wings normally and flying again. But since they always flew with too much lift, bees would soon hit the ceiling and start the cycle all over again.

If you looked at one of the bees and imagined it was a miniature kangaroo and that gravity was upside down for it, well that would help describe the bees' pattern as they bounced from collision with the ceiling to collision with the ceiling and slowly made their way all over the ceiling of our church with no apparent rhyme nor reason to their journey.

The only variation from that bump-fall-fly, bump-fall-fly pattern was when, once in awhile, a bump sort of discombobulated a bee and he couldn't get his wings going fast enough. When that happened, he just dropped like a rock to the floor, or to what ever object or person was directly below. He may have dropped like a rock, but the bee wasn't a rock. He was a bee, complete with stinger and all.

I heard lots of oh's and loud gasps from the ladies when a bee dropped suddenly on to them. Now, in our church, the women were supposed to keep silent in the church, just like the apostle Paul said. But there was no way even the most devout lady was gonna keep quiet when they had a bee in their bonnet, quite literally.

The other thing I heard frequently during the sermon was a deep "whump." You see, the guys might have been listening to the sermon, but many of them also kept their eyes on the bees above them. They usually had their Bibles open, but they liked to keep their Bibles clean, so they kept a hymnal open too. Countless bees were squashed between "Wounded For Me" and "Now I Belong To Jesus." Our hymnals have the grease spots to prove it. The men got pretty good at whumping falling bees right out of the air.

Now Colby and I never whumped bees with our hymnals, because if we made any loud noises, both of our dads gave us the evil eye and we got quiet real quick like. But that doesn't mean Colby kept still. Heck, nothing could keep him still clear through a church service. Well, almost nothing could.

There was one summer Sunday I'll never forget. Since Colby and I couldn't whump bees we just tried to ignore them.

Colby always said, "Odds are only two in a thousand that they'll drop right on us."

My reply was usually, "Then some time between 6 and 16 years old we'll get hit—odds are!"

This particular summer Sunday was the day Colby, the gambler, broke even. We were still singing the hymn just before the sermon when a bee had a bad collision with the ceiling and dropped right on top of Colby's shoe. Before he could sweep it away with his hand, he felt it crawling up his leg just above his sock.

I wasn't quite getting the picture of what was happening, until I noticed that Colby looked liked rigor mortis was setting in.

Before the song finished, I leaned over and whispered to Colby, "Hey Col, what's wrong?"

Only his lips moved, but I heard the words, "Bee went up my pants leg."

We had to quickly get this conversation ended before the song ended because the sermon was next and things would get too quiet to whisper.

I leaned toward Colby again and whispered, "Just smash it real quick like and it won't even get a chance to sting you."

"What if its stinger is pointed at my leg when I smash it?"

"Odds are only two in a thousand that it is, so you'll probably be safe. Smash it!"

Where had I heard those words before? Right before Colby shot that arrow straight up (you can read about that in another story).

"It's climbing higher on my leg," was all Colby got out before the hymn, "Leave It There,"   ended. And, that's what Colby had decided to do. He was gonna leave it there, sit very still, and hope it crawled out soon.

Well, the sermon ended and it hadn't crawled out, so Colby sat stock still.

We had communion, and broke the bread and used one cup like you're supposed to do, and the bee didn't crawl out, so Colby sat stock still.

We sang the final song and prayed the closing prayer, and the bee hadn't crawled out, so Colby sat stock still.

People visited and finally all left the church building and the bee hadn't crawled out, so Colby sat stock still.

Now only Colby and I were left in the building. Since we were free to talk, Colby said moving only his lips, "I can still feel it moving around on my leg every time I even wiggle a little."

"Whatcha' gonna do now?" I asked adding, "Just smash the silly thing! Don't let yourself be held captive by a bee. That sounds like something a girl would do."

I had just trod on dangerous ground and I thought I'd better cool it with my suggestions. But evidently I had a goaded Colby enough that he was gonna try something.

Colby, ever so slowly, rose to the standing position with his legs straight, all without moving his lower leg and while the bee still wandered, lost between his leg hairs.

I couldn't resist making a comment at that point, "Your knee's not bent now. He's got a free run up your pant leg to—"

I cut off my sentence as Colby sprinted out of the church and ran across the church yard to his house slamming the door and continuing on to his bedroom. I was right on his tail and had just entered his room as Colby jerked his pants clear off with one giant motion of his arm. Somewhere along the way he had unbuckled his belt and unzipped his pants.

"Did it sting you?" I asked wondering what was up, but delighted that we could finally leave the church house.

"No! And I can't find the doggone thing!"

"Well, turn your pants leg inside out and see if it's still in there. If it is, then smash it!"

"I don't want to hear any more smash it!" Colby said with a voice strained by stress or anger or both.

But Colby did take my advice and turned his pants leg inside out, examining it with a fine tooth comb. He found only one thing, a loose thread from the seam of his pants that dangled down from about the knee to just above his socks. Convinced that there was no bee in his pants, Colby slipped them back on and wiggled his leg around a bit. I knew that he was feeling a tickle on his leg from that thread in his pants because he just shook his head from side to side in disgust.

The bee that wasn't had done what wasn't possible for anything else to do—that is, to keep Colby stock still in church.

4
Duck-Down
Tickle Torture

Colby's Great Aunt, Ethel, wasn't a rich lady by any stretch of the imagination, but she knew a thing or two about luxury. She was an interesting lady who passed on her childhood stories to us—like when she was growing up in west Texas and became friends with Billy the Kid's girlfriend. Those stories weren't all she passed on to Colby. When Colby's great Uncle John had to move for health reasons, Uncle John and Aunt Ethel left their house and much of what was in it to Colby's family. They left Old Nick, the snake killer, too (that's another story you can read about in this book).

Now our favorite luxury that Aunt Ethel left was Colby's bed. It had duck down-filled pillows and a duck down-filled mattress. People pay a lot of money today for down comforters, bed toppers and pillows, but Colby got his for free.

After a long, hard day of swimming and fishing nothing feels better to a couple of boys than to sink into a down mattress while their heads nestle into a down pillow. But, even when a bed is so comfortable that you could just relax and drift away, sometimes two boys spending the night together just can't drift away—at least not for a while.

Colby and I had an understanding with his parents. As long as we stayed in Colby's room and were quiet enough to let them sleep, we could do pretty much anything we could think of. Sometimes it's dangerous to let Colby think of things, because you see one thing that Colby thought of for us to do when we couldn't think of anything else was to torture each other.

It was a while before we resorted to torture as an amusement because Colby's Dad had the complete collection of Tarzan novels by Edgar Rice Burroughs. It took many, many evenings and lazy afternoons together to exhaust all of those exciting stories. Eventually we read all of the Tarzan books and so we started reading through his Dad's complete Zane Grey collection—we read the stories that didn't get too mushy, but there were a lot of those not too mushy ones to read.

At the conclusion of all that reading was when Colby came up with duck-down tickle torture. You might wonder why two young boys were into any kind of torture. That's because you don't know Colby like I knew him (but if you continue reading this book, you will get an inkling). You see, Colby was into pushing the limits of human endurance. He was always trying to see how much he could do or stand—usually of some unpleasant thing. Once he talked me into seeing how much heat we could stand by sitting in his Dad's pickup with the windows up, in the sun on a 100-degree summer afternoon. I'm sure I lost a few brain cells that day—that happens when your temperature gets too high. Then he got me to see how long I could stay under water, how much hissing from a big bull snake I could take (with the big-fanged snake right in front of my face), and finally how much tickle torture I could stand.

Colby got the idea for this game when he learned that you can always pull a down feather from a down pillow or mattress if you start working one out where the final seam ended when the mattress or pillow was sewn up. Colby got so good at it that he could always pull a feather out in two minutes flat or less. But, so what? Whatcha' gonna do with a fuzzy little down feather? As Colby pondered that question with a long "hhhhmmmmm," he absent mindedly rubbed the feather across his face, smiled, and duck-down tickle torture was hatched.

Here's what you need to play the game:

- two bored boys (so bored they're willing to endure torture for entertainment)

- a small down feather (one with an embryonic quill that's still soft and small, but big enough to hold onto)

- a stop watch, or watch with a second hand, to time with

The rules of the game pretty much pertain to the person being tortured. After all, a torturer doesn't usually have to follow any rules or it wouldn't be called torture. We only had one rule for the torturer; all tickling was to be done on the front side of the head from one ear to the other, and not below the chin or above the hairline. The person being tortured had to lie on their back in the "attention" position. Their hands had to stay at their sides and they could not wiggle them. They also were forbidden wiggling parts of their face. They could not try to scratch using lips or tongue and they could not blow on their face or try to blow on the feather—in other words, they just had to lay there and take it.

When the clock started, the torturer began tickling the permitted area with the feather and the torturee tried not to move at all (except to breath). When the torturee moved, wiggled, *etc.*, the clock stopped and their time was recorded. At this point, the torturer and torturee changed places and the new torturee tried to beat the other person's time by lasting longer.

You can see how important it was to develop advanced tickling skills if you wanted to win at this "game." Well, we both became experts in short order. By age fourteen we had mapped all of the nerves of the face more completely than an acupuncturist.

Colby rapidly became an expert torturer. Now I have always been able to stand a lot of tickling, but not the way he delivered it. He knew which areas of the face were so sensitive that running a feather ever so lightly over them left an itch in its wake so unnerving that it would drive a boy crazy. But Colby also knew that itchy-spot knowledge by itself was not enough. As we both developed high levels of itch tolerance, no one place was sensitive enough to guarantee you a win if you tickled there.

Being a real student of this game, Colby deduced that the urge to scratch was proportional to the sums of the squares of each area's itch index. For those not mathematically inclined, let me explain. To make a person really itch, you have to get all of the sensitive areas of the face itching at the same time. If you do, the cumulative itch goes up by a factor of a thousand—heck, I'd say by a factor of a million the way he did it.

Let me illustrate. Imagine that you are lying on a bed, hands at your sides trying not to move at all. Now you tense up a bit as a feather lightly touches your cheek, which was Colby's way of saying to you, "I know that didn't itch at all, but I want your imagination to run wild with thoughts of how bad you are about to itch." And mine did.

Next you feel an itching inside of one ear. It spreads from the ear canal outward until the whole ear itches and your nervous system screams to your brain, "Tell the hands to scratch you fool! Scratch!" This is the time when you try to detach your body from your mind, keeping both in their separate worlds. You do this by thinking intently on something else. By the time your pretty well into thinking about when you made the winning basket at the buzzer, or when you scored the winning touchdown and you recall the exhilaration, right then your entire other ear begins to harmonize with the first ear singing the "Scratch you fool" stanza from a song that you wish to hear not another stanza, not another line, not another measure, not another note!

At this point, when your desire to win collides head on with common sense, if you're a strong person, you continue at bit longer. But, your breathing transitions from equally spaced contractions of your diaphragm to irregular, spasmodic gasps. This is where Colby quickly and cleverly attacks the corner of your mouth, the edge of your nose and your upper lip with quick, deft motions of the feather. The itching explodes to a level where your body starts to quiver so much you think Colby might say you moved, thus ending your turn. That's when a rational thought flashes through your panicking mind. "If I wiggle my nose or make some other token attempt to scratch, it will end my turn but it will not end the torture of the itching. So, I should just scratch!" And you do—for the next fifteen minutes.

As you look at the stop watch, you realize what Colby was able to accomplish in three minutes with a small down feather and you begin thinking that the army should hire Colby for special ops training or maybe the CIA for making the bad guys talk using duck-down tickle torture.

5
The Longbowmen

Colby and I had never seen a tree quite like that one. But after we identified it, each cut a limb from it, and completed our projects, the results were beyond our wildest dreams. We had become like those most dreaded British warriors of the 14th century, the longbowmen.

After Colby's family moved to the little white house, Colby and I had 160 acres of property behind his Mom and Dad's house to explore. Most of this acreage was wooded. Near the back of the property on the east side of the land was a creek and on its banks was a large evergreen tree. The tree limbs, needles, and even its bark were unlike the evergreens we knew so well, Douglas fir, white fir, noble fir, hemlock, spruce, sugar pine, ponderosa pine—we just didn't know what this particular tree was. Furthermore, something about the tree captured our imaginations. This tree was special—we knew it, but couldn't quite put our finger on the reason why.

One day Colby, his Dad and I drove in their old pickup up the barely passable road from Colby's house to the creek to haul some wood. We asked his Dad if he knew what kind of tree it was that grew there on the banks of the little creek. Now being an experienced lumber-mill worker who had cut and planed just about every kind of evergreen that grew in the Pacific Northwest, he answered us saying, "That's a yew tree."

Colby asked the question that had been weighing heavy on our minds, "Is there anything special about a yew tree?"

"Son," his Dad said in a quiet, respectful voice, "that's the tree they make bows from."

I piped up, "Really?"

"Really," Colby's Dad answered. "Some of the finest bows ever made have come from yew trees."

Well I looked at Colby and he looked at me. Both of us were smiling because we knew that in a few days both of us would have one of those "finest bows ever made."

Now I'm gonna give you some facts here that I want you to remember. At the time, Colby and I were completely unaware of these historical facts, and regardless of whether it was coincidence, providence, or satanic influence (sometimes I am convinced it was the latter), there was a guiding hand at work insuring that the weapons we made were as deadly as any bow ever made.

When the longbow was introduced by the English military around 1250 A.D., warfare changed for all time. You see, by 100 years later the English longbowmen made bows that were from six to six and one-half feet long from yew wood. These bows had a 30-inch draw and could fire an arrow up to 360 yards.

To qualify as an archer, the English bowmen had to be able to sustain a shooting rate of one arrow every three seconds for three minutes and be able to hit a man-sized target 200 yards away. When a whole battery of English archers was doing this, they took out knights in armor, their horses, and crossbowmen before the enemy was even within striking distance.

The English longbow was sort of like the German battleship Bismarck. The Bismarck fired on ships (like the Hood) 15 miles away, clear over the horizon, and sunk them before they could even see the Bismarck (at least that's what Johnny Horton said in his song, Sink the Bismarck). I'll bet that was how the French felt—like the Hood—when in 1346 A.D. an army of only 12,000 Englishmen defeated a French force of more than 50,000 at Crecy, using the longbow for tactical advantage.

Even beyond 200 yards, in fact as far as 300 yards away, a group of English archers could shoot rapid volleys with their longbows toward a group of advancing soldiers and make them look like porcupines.

The longbow was the ICBM of the middle Ages and Colby and I were just about to each own one. Colby grabbed a hacksaw after we got back to the house and we headed back toward the creek where the beautiful specimen of *taxus brevifolia* was growing. We each carefully sawed off one limb of our own choice.

I picked a section of a branch about three inches thick on one end, tapering to two and one-half inches thick on the other, about six and one-half feet long, and having a slight natural curvature to it. The curve would make it easier to string the bow when I was ready for that. Colby cut off a branch similar in size and length.

I took my knife and carved off nearly one half of what was to be the back side of the bow. On the other side, I removed only the bark, then I proceeded to make that bow as smooth as possible by scraping it with my knife, and finally, by using fine-grained sand paper. On both ends, I whittled out little grooves that would hold my bowstring taut after I strung the bow. In so doing, I had in ignorance used the yew branch just as a master bow maker would have done—heartwood to the back, sap wood on the front for maximum power.

Down at the hardware store we bought a roll of woven nylon string and some target arrows for both Colby and me. I took three 10-foot strands of string and braided them to create a tough bowstring that was thick enough so I wouldn't cut my fingers when I pulled it back as far as I could (which for me was about a 30-inch draw). By that time, the wood in our two bows was pretty dry, so we strung our bows and headed for a vacant field that was about 150 yards long. It was adjacent to another field that extended another 200 yards further in the same direction.

The Moment of truth was at hand. I notched an arrow, pointed it down the full 350-yard flight path that the adjacent fields provided, raised the bow to a 45 degree angle and released my grip on the bowstring. There was a powerful "twang" from the string, the bow recoiled slightly in my hand, and the arrow just disappeared. It was moving far too fast for the human eye to track.

Colby, who had been waiting for his turn to shoot, just un-notched his arrow and hollered, "Man! Did you see that?"

"No, after I let go, it was just gone!"

Already on the run down the field, Colby yelled back at me, "Let's go find it before I shoot mine—so we know about how far these arrows are gonna go!"

After about five minutes, we found my arrow buried deep into the ground. I stepped off the distance as we returned. As I counted the last few steps out loud, Colby's head jerked a bit with each number—"294, 295, 296, 297, 298". We had proven that our longbows were nearly as powerful as the English archers' bows, but the pull was light enough so boys our age could draw them fully.

Now that we were back at our starting point, Colby wanted to shoot his arrow 300 yards too. So he raised his bow, inclining it to 45 degrees, then to 60 degrees, finally all the way to 90 degrees, and turned the bowstring loose. That arrow was gone—out of sight—straight up!

"Man, are you crazy?" I said strongly implying that Colby had lost his marbles. I feared one of us would soon have a blow hole on the top of our heads like a whale.

"I don't even know which way to run!" I complained to Colby.

Looking calm and cool Colby chose only to make a statistical evaluation of our situation, "Just stay where you are, the odds are only about two chances in a thousand that we'll be hit. So stay coo—"

He was interrupted by a nerve shattering "thunk" as the arrow buried eight inches into the ground, just 15 feet to my right.

"See," Colby said reassuringly, "no sweat. Odds are we'll be safe."

"You're darn right I'll be safe, 'cause I'm exiting this field right now!"

"Thwang," Colby released another arrow straight up and looked at me with a smirk on his face and said, "Which way you gonna go to exit?"

He had made his point. I thought to myself, "No direction I go will be safe until that arrow—"

"Chunk!" his second arrow buried half its shaft right between the two of us.

Just then I thought how thankful I was that Colby wasn't one of those journeymen archers that could shoot 20 arrows per minute—the odds would have changed. I also thought of something that would give me an edge in case Colby let fly another vertical shot. I grabbed a handful of dust and threw it high into the air. It drifted to the southeast. Just then I saw Colby release an arrow slightly off vertical toward the northwest. Colby had taken my way out away. Running upwind would no longer be a way to put some distance between me and the point of impact. I had to wait this one out too.

"Thoink," the last arrow glanced off a rock and lay somehow unbroken on the ground practically on my foot.

Each arrow Colby released was untrackable with the human eye. All we could do was wait while visions of my foot being pinned to the ground by a feathered wooden spike or wearing a feather-tipped epaulet ran through my mind.

I had just about had it at that point and was just about tell Colby to go down field 75 yards and put an apple on his head when I thought, "Knowing Colby, he'll probably do it."

Well I refrained from asking Colby to do that William Tell thing and, much to my relief, he finally refrained from his game of Russian longbow roulette. Now, Colby and I made other weapons during our years together, like our reproduction of the sling David killed Goliath with, but none were as impressive as those long pieces of yew wood that turned two boys into the longbowmen.

Limestone Caves Lore

From the time Colby and I were just little squirts we had heard rumors from many sources that there were limestone caves on top of the mountain above Kerby. When we were about ten, we met an old geologist who told us that, not only were their limestone caves up there, but there was so much limestone that he thought the rock formation, which was largely underground, joined with Oregon Caves formation ten miles away.

Needless to say our eagerness to find and explore those caves soon sent us up into mountains to find them. As it turned out, it was easy to find them if you found the right old overgrown logging road—it led you all the way there. A short, but sometimes steep, three-mile hike up that road would take you to the main caves at the top of the mountain.

The huge rock spire on top of the mountain had a large cave at its base. This cave was nearly twelve feet high at the mouth, but it soon slimmed down to some really small tunnels that were hard to fully explore—especially if you had claustrophobia. High up on the eastern side of the rock was a cave you had to climb to reach. It had a nice cavern a short ways back in. The cavern had some old dates written on its wall—one said 1915. If you looked really closely, some very faint petroglyphs were still visible in the rocks of that cavern. We guessed that Indians had made them, but we had no idea how old they really were.

On the hike up to the caves you passed two water holes. The second one had a spring that burbled right out of a rock on the side of the mountain. It ran year round and provided pure, cool, refreshing drinking water to Colby and me on nearly every trip. The spring ran into a small pond that served as a watering hole for all sorts of wild life on the mountain—deer, quail, grouse, squirrels, rabbits, coyotes, and in the '50s, bobcats and cougars.

The stories I could tell of what we did there are many, but the three stories I remember best, for reasons you will soon understand, I have called simply, "Limestone Caves Lore."

6
Claustrophobia Cavern

With each trip to the caves, that foot-high opening at the back of the big cave increasingly captured the imaginations of Colby and me. But, it raised questions too. What was on the other side of it? Could we actually squeeze under that overhanging rock without getting stuck so we could see what was on the other side? Was this the way to the big cavern we heard rumors of from the old timers in the area?

When we had peered along the floor underneath the overhanging chunk of limestone, what we saw resembled a giant vise turned on its side, slightly open, just waiting to squeeze to death any boys foolish enough to try crawling between its jaws. At the end of the overhang was a big rock that jutted upward effectively blocking our view of whatever lay beyond and thus creating an intriguing mystery for two boys.

Now, certain types of confining environs give me claustrophobia. Not so for Colby. If there was enough oxygen to keep him conscious, then he thought even the smallest hole or box was a fine place to be.

One day when Colby and I decided, spur-of-the-moment, to trek up the mountain to the limestone caves, curiosity got the best of Colby. Flat on his belly, he started army crawling under the overhang, a distance of about twelve feet, to see what was really back there. Unfortunately, the spur-of-the-moment decision left us without a light. Between the two of us we couldn't even come up with as much as a single match. So with only the ambient light, Colby inched his way under the big rock, through the death vise, to the rock that blocked our view, and up into the dark unknown.

Though I wasn't fond of the idea of crawling under that big rock, I was even less fond of being thought a chicken. Now, I knew Colby wouldn't call me a chicken to my face, but I'd be able to see it in his eyes—I'd do almost anything to avoid that. So, I started crawling on my belly toward either the greatest discovery a boy spelunker can make or sheer terror—I didn't know which. But, I did know to keep my head down. If your bottom lip wasn't dragging in the dirt, the underside of that rock would really give you a headache.

Within a couple of minutes, both of us were perched on top of the rock which had hitherto blocked our view. Now, something else blocked our view—darkness. The sound of our echoing voices told us there was a cavern straight ahead, but to climb down the other side of the rock that we sat on would be sheer folly because, try as we may, we could see absolutely nothing as we peered into the darkness before us.

If Colby and I proceeded we might topple down into the bowels of the earth or encounter some other terror only a boy's imagination can conjure up. We agreed that it wasn't worth the risk at that time.

"Next time we'll bring a light," Colby said emphatically. "This might be the big cavern we've heard rumors about."

"Sure," I agreed. But the only thing I was really "sure" about was the urge to move toward that narrow slight of light along the floor behind us and to slither out to the main cave to daylight where the air and the breathing were free and easy.

The next time we went up to the caves we did bring a light, one flashlight. That wasn't all we brought though. We brought Don and Vaughn B, twins who were my close friends. But, Colby knew them too because they used to attend the church without a Sunday school.

The twins were a constant amazement to me. Though Don and Vaughn were wrestlers, not basketball players, we still played a lot of pick-up basketball games with them. Neither of the twins was basketball-talented in the traditional sense, but you really didn't want to play against these guys. Over and over I would see one of them just throw they ball at some odd angle without even looking. Sure enough, the other one was there, usually wide open for a shot. Their means of communication still remains a mystery to me. Some time I'll have to tell you about Don and me riding our motorcycles through the halls of Grants Pass High School, popping the clutch and doing wheelies as we roared through. I don't know if the janitor ever got all the black rubber marks off from the floor. When we graduated you could still see them faintly underneath layers of wax. But, that's another story for another time.

Back to the limestone caves—the four of us found ourselves in the big cave at the base of the rock with one flashlight, looking at the horizontally running slit we were about to slide through to adventures unknown. My stomach tightened a little, but hey, I had done this before, at least part of it, so I figured I could handle anything Don and Vaughn could handle—anything Colby could handle, well that was a different story.

We started crawling single file with me in the rear. Colby was in the lead with the flashlight crawling up the blocking rock as I was still squeezing through the death vise. My angst was temporarily quelled as I heard Colby exclaim, "There is a cavern here! It's not huge, but it sure goes up a long way," he added.

When I topped the rock and peered into the cavern I saw Colby shining the light upward.

"I can't see the top of the chimney," Colby said while looking intently upward. "You guys feel anything?" he asked.

"I don't know about feeling anything, but something sure stinks in here," I answered, beginning to feel a bit uneasy despite the comfortable size of the cavern.

The sides of the chimney extended far upward tapering in slightly with height. They were covered with a wet slimy substance—probably algae or mold. I could feel occasional puffs of foul air coming down upon us. Colby evidently felt the breeze too and shouted a warning, "I'm going to turn the light out for a few seconds to see if there is any light coming in from the top. Maybe there's an opening into this cave from the top of the rock formation."

Simultaneously, Don and Vaughn said, "Good idea."

"Yeah," I replied, but that affirmation was a much more positive statement than my jittery emotions were stating to me.

As our eyes adjusted to the darkness, Don spoke first, "Isn't that some light coming in way up there directly above us?"

It was very dim, but it did appear to be light and we all felt an occasional downdraft on our skin indicating that air was coming in through the chimney above.

"If that's light from the outside, then it's got to be from an opening about 300 feet above us," Colby reasoned, because the rock face of the limestone formation extended upward to a height of about 300 feet above the cave where we had entered.

With no further discussion, assuming we would follow, Colby started climbing one of the chimney walls that appeared to have the best foot and hand holds. Don and Vaughn fell in behind Colby and began the ascent up the chimney wall, trying without success to avoid the slime that was growing there.

"Shine the light down here for a second so I can see how to get started up. It's too dark to see anything when the light is shining up," I complained.

Colby gave me enough light to reach Vaughn's feet, then we all began the ascent in earnest—four brave young spelunkers climbing a slime-covered, three hundred foot high wall with virtually no equipment while we breathed foul air—maybe there were only three brave spelunkers.

To me the air began to feel dense, like you had to suck hard through a straw to get anything and when you got some of it, you just wanted to exhale that stuff as quickly as possible.

It wasn't until two more decades passed that I found out I'm allergic to molds. They give me a heavy-chest kind of feeling. Sometimes I start wheezing and, in extremely moldy places, I have had asthma attacks. All I knew at the time was that sucking in the foul air was getting harder and the stench more nauseating with each step upward. Breathing was like slurping up a putrid slime shake through a tiny straw.

It was at this juncture that the light went out. Colby, after rattling the light and clicking its on-off button repeatedly yelled, "Can't get the light to work! I think it's shot!"

Trying to keep my mind off the rising feeling of smothering, I thought about another, more pleasant time, that we experienced total darkness. A few years earlier Colby and I had toured the Oregon Caves together. The tour guide gathered everyone in the middle of a large cavern, then had the cave lighting system turned off. He continued his lecture for three or four minutes while our eyes dilated maximally in the total darkness. Then the guide had instructed us to partner with someone near our own height and stand face to face about a foot apart.

Colby and I were almost nose to nose when the guide struck a single match in this cavern which was about forty yards across. It looked like broad daylight when the match lit. Colby's pupils seemed to fill his entire eye for a split second and they then shrank to near pin-head size as the light overcame the darkness.

Now, I know that darkness is just the absence of light. You learn that in elementary physics. You even learn it in theology classes. For the first time I had an inkling of what the Bible meant when it said Jesus was the light of the world. Without light we are blind and groping for what we're hoping for, but only finding whatever we happen to bump in to.

But to me, somewhere on the wall of a foul smelling cavern, the darkness seemed to have the properties of matter—it took up space, it had weight, and that weight was crushing me. I slurped, but it was as if some of that slime had plugged my straw and nothing came through.

At that moment, in a split second, sheer claustrophobic panic hit. Now, panic can cause you to do some dumb things, but sheer claustrophobic panic leaves no room for intellect, reason, or common sense. Your IQ simply drops to zero in an instant. I had never felt this kind of panic before and was ill equipped to deal with it. So, I simply turned and leaped into the darkness. That was the quickest way back to the light.

Keep in mind that we had been slowly climbing up the chimney wall for quite a while. Since the light had been carried above me by Colby, I hadn't looked down since we started our ascent. How high up were we? Ten feet? One hundred feet? I hadn't a clue. The single motive that dominated me was to get out of the cave and into broad daylight taking the shortest path possible—that's exactly what I proceeded to do.

While in the air, I had no idea how long it would be before I hit bottom, but I had an idea that it was going to hurt. On the way down, a recently recorded mental image of the cavern's floor flashed through my mind—whaddya' know, a rational thought at last. The floor was composed of about two-thirds uneven rock and about one-third fairly flat dirt. My fall lasted long enough for me to utter a desperate prayer, "Please let both feet hit on something level!" I felt that a positive answer to that prayer was my only chance to avoid serious injury.

Based upon the length of my fall, I was probably only about twenty feet up when I bailed. But, God was both merciful and gracious. By that I mean that I didn't get what I deserved and I got something that I didn't deserve. Both feet hit on flat surfaces, one on dirt another on a flat rock.

With my adrenaline spigot wide open, I was able to completely absorb the shock of landing with my newly acquired super leg strength, and then shoot up the blocking rock, dive head first into the death vise, explode from the death vise like a shell out of a canon, and finally sprint to the mouth of the cave with super speed.

The complete sequence from the jump to exiting the mouth of the cave took no more than five or six seconds. I know that is not humanly possible for anyone, except maybe Clark Kent, but a person in full panic is more than a mere human being. If you suspect that you see such a person, my advice to you is just stay out of their way.

Colby, Don and Vaughn had all heard a solid thump, some sliding noises, and then running footsteps. As their eyes adjusted to make maximal use of the tiny sliver of light leaking in from under the overhang, they looked around. Since they couldn't see me, and got no reply when addressing me, they were concerned because it did not seem possible for me to disappear so quickly.

Convinced something dreadful had happened to me, they managed to climb down and look and feel around for me in the cavern. Finding no dead or injured body, they backtracked out of the cave.

Seeing me standing in the mouth of the cave, Don ran up to me and asked, "You OK?"

I answered with the only answer any self-respecting boy could give, "Sure."

But what I really was "sure" of was that they could see they whites showing all around my eyes as well as the fact that I was still hyperventilating.

The moral of this story is that no one should ever go exploring caves without the proper equipment and, if you feel uncomfortable in tight places, then don't explore caves at all unless you enjoy the feeling of suffocation. Remember claustrophobia kills—first the intellect so it can then have the whole body. Only by God's grace and watch-care did it not get my body that day in claustrophobia cavern.

7
Shrinkwrapped

I don't know about Colby, but I'll never forget the pain, the feeling of defilement, and the mad frenzy that drove us to do what we would ordinarily never do, even on a dare, on the day we got shrinkwrapped.

We were experiencing part of that notable period of global cooling which lasted from the 1940's through the late 1960's. It gave us one winter so cold and snowy that Colby and I were unable to get to the top of the mountain to the limestone caves for most of the winter—not even for some cheap entertainment (you can read about the nature of our cheap amusement in another story). Consequently, late winter left us hankering for rock cliffs, caves, and the fun of climbing the mountain to get to the big limestone formation perched so nobly atop the mountain overlooking the Illinois River Valley.

Our hankering soon turned into a trek up the mountain. As we started encountering mud and patches of snow Colby remarked, "You know, we've never been up here when there was this much snow on the ground. No telling what we might find." As it turned out—we didn't tell.

"Yeah. The snow's a good reason to take the lower fork and check out the cave down below. Probably less snow down there," I surmised. "We sure wouldn't want to slide off a glacier on the big rock and fall over the cliff."

Now, about a year after we discovered the big limestone formation with numerous caves in it, we had found a second large outcropping of this huge, mostly subterranean, chunk of limestone. This outcropping lay farther down, on the back side of the mountain. A deserted logging road, partly overgrown by forest, led right up to the cave that I was recommending we visit today.

The really neat thing about this cave is that it went clear through the rock, which was some 50 yards across, and came out on the other side. The cave was large and it had a dogleg halfway in that kept you from being able to see the light at the other end of the cave. The dogleg produced an area of near total darkness that a spelunking boy would encounter shortly after entering either end of the cave. The dark area proved very costly to Colby and me on this fateful day.

As I said, it was late winter (actually early March). It still looked a lot like mid-winter in the mountains. But to Colby and me, and to something like maybe a hibernating bear, I'm sure this winter seemed to have lasted long enough. A bear would think it was time to go foraging for food just as we were foraging for fun.

For Colby and me the trek up to the caves was ill-timed in one sense, but well timed for sunshine. Today was a blue-sky, fifty-degree day up at the caves. While standing in the sun you could feel some warmth. For that, Colby and I would soon be very thankful.

As we made our descent on the lower logging road, down from the ridgeline to our destination, we were making observations of all that was happening on the mountain after the hard winter. There were signs of the coming spring, but the claws of winter were also digging in for winter's last stand.

"Creek sure is running high. We can't even find enough water to get a drink here during summer," Colby commented.

"That's not the only difference between now and summer," I added. "Even when it runs during the summer, it's almost too warm to drink. I just stuck my hand in and it's about the same temperature as the melting snow feeding it," my meteorologically oriented mind voiced.

"Come on, I see the cave," Colby excitedly exclaimed as he picked up his pace to a trot.

The road angled slightly uphill, and then came to an abrupt ending point surrounded by limestone outcroppings. On our left was a short, steep hill. Just over the crest of that hill yawned the upper palate of the cave's mouth.

As you know, I can get claustrophobic at times, so visions of the cave as a mouth about to devour us did flit across my mind. But, as things turned out, it was not the cave that was intent on eating us.

We scrambled up the hill and, at last, Colby and I stood at the entrance to an afternoon of pure boyhood delight, or so we thought.

Colby entered first with me tagging tentatively along behind him. About twenty feet in we entered the dark portion of this end of the cave. While we could still make out the general contours of the cave walls, we could not see any details of the cave wall surface. It was at this point that we began to play our role in the making of the horror film entitled, "Shrinkwrapped."

I say shrinkwrapped because that's what appeared to be happening as the lining of the cave wall collapsed tightly around Colby and me. We felt like we were being shrinkwrapped in black plastic. Some ghoul was running a pump that sucked every bit of air out until the black lining conformed to our bodies' contours—it was a precise conformity.

I felt smothered, but that feeling turned out not to be a big deal because I didn't feel that way for long, maybe just a tenth of a second, before that feeling was overshadowed by another. Evidently Colby felt that overshadowing feeling too because he began screaming at the same instant that my vocal chords involuntarily maxed out.

You know that Preparation H commercial that talks about, "The burning and the itching!" I can tell you that hemorrhoids are a picnic compared to the itching and the burning we felt.

What had evidently happened was that a bear had used the cave to hibernate for most of that winter. He had left the cave a few weeks before we entered and he had a really bad case of fleas. Do you know how fast fleas multiply? Even if he only had about 100 fleas on him, given the reproduction rate of fleas, those 100 fleas could become 2.5 million in a short time.

You can probably imagine now how many voracious fleas lined the walls of that cave. In a moment, in the twinkling of an eye, millions of starved fleas had leaped in perfect unison to devour the only warm blooded creatures within leaping distance, Colby and me.

Wherever bare skin was exposed, they bit immediately. Wherever there were openings in our clothing (pant legs, *etc.*) they bit almost immediately. Wherever our clothing was of a coarse weave, they bit nearly almost immediately. There was a progression here that horrified us as we took this biting progression to its logical and mathematical limits. Where would they be in five more seconds? Even now, I don't want to think about that.

Now the fleas really didn't want to kill Colby and me. They just wanted to suck all of the nutrients from every drop of blood that coursed through every blood vessel in our bodies. They pretty near did!

With the bite count going well into the thousands, we were sure to catch whatever these evil little leaping, blood-sucking boogers were carrying. My mind quickly listed all of the diseases that fleas can carry: Typhus, not a big deal; Plague, that's nasty and about 10 people in the U.S. get it every year; Bubonic Plague, the black death—please no; Pneumonic Plague, anything but one of those suffocating diseases!

My mind accelerated through a list of the symptoms of these diseases: fever, chills, headaches, skin lesions, chest pain, delirium, bleeding organs, death! My thought volume crescendoed when my mind hit bleeding organs and death.

I don't know about Colby, but I was ready to do anything to be rid of this black, chitinic skin I seemed to have grown. This was a life and death situation and desperate measures were called for.

It seems Colby and I both had the same idea as we exited the cave at a sprint. As we ran, popped buttons flew, then items of clothing flew—every single item of clothing flew. A trail of abandoned garments led from the cave to the creek.

In less than ten seconds we had completely stripped and two boys' bodies, white from the long winter—at least the parts that weren't still black with fleas were white—leaped into the snow fed stream, submerged themselves completely in the frigid water without so much as a "Brrr that's cold" and scrubbed furiously as two trails of small black dots flowed downstream.

The fish were well fed that day, that is, if trout like fleas. Later Colby and I wondered about trout and fleas but we could think of no real way to test our hypothesis—at least no way I wanted to try.

With the worst of the panic past, Colby and I sat in the slightly warm sun in the balmy fifty-degree air to dry and thaw out. As we slowly dried and looked at the areas of our most exposed skin that were glowing pink from the thousands of bites we had suffered, Colby spoke up, "If Mom asks, and if we're still not symptomatic, let's just tell her we got sunburned."

I concurred with the lie. The truth was too embarrassing and too horrible.

We then sat silently waiting for the onset of chills, fever and headaches. We both were shaking, but I assumed that was because we were almost frozen to death, not because we were getting sick.

After a long while, we began violently shaking each item of clothing. We then meticulously examined every square inch of fabric on every garment before putting anything back on. Somehow we had completely eradicated the fleas from both of our bodies and from our clothing.

Though Colby and I cringed each time we envisioned a disease-ridden bear occupying that cave, and though we continued waiting for disease symptoms to start, by God's grace, we never experienced any of the symptoms of flea-carried diseases. We were both thankful that we caught none of those dread diseases that we may have been exposed to on that day when we got shrinkwrapped.

8
Cheap Entertainment

A ten-cent box of matches, a Sears and Roebuck catalog, and a hike up to the limestone caves—for two boys you just can't find any better cheap entertainment.

Colby and I grew up during that moderately long period of global cooling that occurred near the middle of the 20th-century. For southern Oregon this impacted our climate somewhat—it generally gave us dry weather until about Thanksgiving, then the rains set in. From the beginning of December on an early snow was a distinct possibility.

Either the rain or the snow would suffice. It didn't really matter which to Colby and me. Our primary concern was that we didn't want to be charged with burning up Josephine County, so we waited for wet and cool conditions before getting our supplies ready. A big box of matches could usually be begged from Colby's Mom—she trusted us too much. Even if we had to buy them, a dime got you a big box of good quality matches—the kind with a good striker on the side and match heads that lit on the first try. An outdated Sears catalog could always be scrounged from around the house—everybody had them in abundance in those days.

The third ingredient, a trek to the caves, and then what we did there, comprise the heart of this story.

I told you already that the caves consist of multiple outcroppings of limestone mostly atop a big mountain overlooking the Illinois River valley. What I haven't provided is a detailed description of the main rock—the big spire perched on the very top of the mountain.

If you approach the peak of the limestone rock from the back side of the mountain, you can practically walk right up to the peak. Now there are some four- or five-foot high rocks to get across, but no real climbing is involved in getting to the peak. But what you see there is enough to take a young boy's breath away. When you walk right out to the edge of the rock, you can look down the face of a 300-foot high limestone cliff. The rock forming the cliff actually leans out a little so that you feel like you're hanging out into space when you look down from the top.

If you drop a rock off the peak of the limestone rock, it will hit the ground about 30 or 40 feet out from the base of the rock (that's how much the rock leans out). Below the limestone cliff, the mountainside is also very steep (about a 60-degree slope). The steepness of the mountain slope makes the cliff feel about twice as high as it really is. Standing on top of the rock face made Colby and me feel like we were on top of the world—at least of our world.

This was the perfect place for our afternoon of amusement. We would need all 300 feet of the cliff's height plus a hundred feet or so of the steep mountainside to provide the height we needed for our activities.

There was a very real danger of falling up where Colby and I played. You just couldn't afford to do that from this height 'cause if you fell off the cliff you would strike a glancing blow off the side of the mountain 300 feet below and then bounce all the way down the mountainside to the little town of Kerby in the bottom of the valley. We didn't think anyone could possibly survive all that, so we looked around for some way to ensure we wouldn't fall.

Now the main reason we were so concerned about falling is derived from the fact that both Colby and I needed to lean our heads out three feet over the cliff edge to have our fun and games. I found a perfect way to do that without any fear of falling. There was a place right at the pinnacle of the rock where it had a crack on the top about a foot back from the edge of the cliff. The crack was about 6 inches wide and about 6 feet long and went down deep enough so that if you turned your feet so your toes were pointed out to the sides and jammed your feet down in the crack, the rock braced you all the way up to about mid thigh. That left the whole upper part of your body free to lean as far over the edge as you desired. You couldn't lean so far that you would fall, because the soles of your shoes were wedged in so tightly that you could hardly pull your shoes loose even when you wanted to. The crack was perfect for holding two boys in perfect safety.

Having your feet turned sideways with your toes pointing straight out to the sides is not very comfy. Whenever Colby and I used the crack to hold us, I had to take a short break to rest my ankles every 15 minutes for so. Colby had to do the same almost every half hour. Now Vaughn B could have stayed in that crack all day—it was his natural pose. When Vaughn walked up to you, as he stopped he always rotated his feet so his toes pointed straight out to the sides. That's how they remained until Vaughn walked away. Too bad Colby and I couldn't borrow Vaughn's ankles for a day.

On this particular early December day, we had a light dusting of snow at Colby's house, so we grabbed our matches and a catalog and headed up the mountain for the caves. At the top of the mountain about two inches of snow had fallen, so Colby was sure there was no way we could burn up the county—we had been paranoid of burning up things unintentionally ever since that last day we played the game, firebug (you can read about that in another story).

We each slid down into a section of the crack, struck the Vaughn B pose, and pushed our shoes in until they were firmly stuck. Colby laid the box of matches as well as the Sears and Roebuck catalog on a little rock bench between us that looked tailor-made for this purpose. Then we got down to the business at hand.

The first matter of business was for me to test the wind. I ripped a page out of the catalog and very carefully folded that world-champion paper glider pattern that I had memorized. I then struck a match and lit the little airplane's tail and launched it in its kamikaze flight. The glider started off nicely, sailing smoothly about 30 feet or so out from the rock, and only descending a little in so doing. But, it did have the telltale smoke trail behind it, which was emerging right from behind the little orange flame that was eating ever deeper into the rear end of my glider.

When the paper airplane's wings became sufficiently shortened, it began to lose lift. At that moment, the nose pointed downward and the little glider went into a corkscrew-shaped death spiral. At the end of the corkscrew, some red hot embers and a little unburned paper sizzled ever so briefly in the snow more than 350 feet below Colby and me.

Colby and I cheered for the brave little plane. Then we cheered for the pilot (who ever he was). Then we cheered for the sheer joy of making little planes fly so far to their doom. Finally we cheered because we still had 853 pages of catalog and 650 matches left in the box.

Much later, after we used all of the paper, the matches, and all the daylight that we dare, Colby and I yanked our shoes loose from the depths of the crack and headed down the mountain, thankful that we had access to such wonderful cheap entertainment.

9
Kangaroo Court For
A Grasshopper

In my mind the grasshopper was guilty—as guilty as sin. As the prosecuting attorney my only decision was whether or not to charge him, or her as the case may be, with a capital offense. With Judge Colby presiding, I decided to go for the gallows in this kangaroo court for a grasshopper.

Speaking of gallows, you know which country's national anthem (unofficial, yet *de facto*, national anthem) talks about hanging someone for a capital offense? Here's a hint—it's not a Muslim country. It's Australia. Guessed it didn't you, or did you?

You see, Banjo Paterson—now there was a man's poet—used the phrase "waltzing Matilda" as a play on words meaning three different things over the course of the song. Initially the swagman's pack swings to and fro as he walks. It's waltzing with him. Then in the third stanza, up rides the squatter, down come the troopers, and the inquiry is made as to whose jumbuck is in the swagman's tucker bag. The squatter implies that the swagman stole the jumbuck from him and when the squatter says, "You'll come a waltzing Matilda with me," he is talking about the swagman swinging to and fro from the noose on the gallows.

"Waltzing Matilda" played in repeat mode through my mind as I built my ironclad case against the grasshopper fact by fact, precept upon precept, case citation by case citation.

My little sister, Maria, was only about five years old while Colby and I were nine or 10. Maria was very softhearted and would readily come to the legal defense of any unfortunate insect that our kangaroo court drug before Judge Colby. Yes, Maria was a public defender we could always count on for a spirited defense.

Now this case was a bit unusual because the grasshopper's alleged crime was against Colby. So, he was presiding over a trial in which he was the plaintiff. That's not legally kosher, but a judge like Colby didn't care about such trivial deviations from the protocols of jurisprudence. He just walked into the courtroom (his Dad's shop) and took his place behind the bench (his Dad's workbench), and banged the sledge hammer on the old anvil calling the court to order and causing our ears to ring.

As prosecuting attorney, I had Colby sworn in and he took his seat on the witness stand." Mr. Colby," I asked, "did this grasshopper spit tobacco juice on you today?"

"Yes, he did. Got the vile stuff all over my thumb!" Colby responded.

I probed further, "Were you doing anything to provoke the grasshopper?"

"Nope. Just picked him up to examine him," Colby answered confidently.

Maria jumped up and objected, "Maybe the grasshopper didn't want to be picked up. You can't just pick up anybody you want to!"

From the witness stand Colby quickly responded with his ruling, "Objection overruled! It's not your turn yet so sit down!"

Maria looked at the thread-shackled grasshopper sitting beside her and the corners of her mouth drooped. Having defended clients in this kangaroo court before, she was starting to lose hope for her case, but not losing her determination to fight for this little insect. She sat quietly and tried to wait for her turn.

I resumed my questioning of Colby, "Now tell the Court just how you picked up this grasshopper."

"Well, I reached down from behind him and slowly and gently grasped him between my thumb and forefinger. Then I turned him so I could look into his face," Colby explained.

"What happened next?" I asked.

"The little booger spit tobacco juice all over my thumb," complained Colby.

"At this point, had you done anything at all to provoke such a criminal assault," I asked, clearly violating a half dozen rules for questioning witnesses.

"No, I just opened his wings to see what color they were," Colby answered again confidently.

Now Maria was boiling, I could see that as I knew quite well both my little sister's hot buttons and her responses to them being pushed. She jumped up yelling, "You were hurting him! You can't just go pulling on his wings like that!"

In unison Colby and I said, "Sit down, you'll get your turn!"

At this juncture I dismissed the witness and Colby sat down behind the bench, again becoming judge Colby and banging the sledge hammer on the anvil to drive that point home.

I summarized my case, "Judge, the prosecution has shown that without provocation this grasshopper committed a capital offense by assaulting you with tobacco juice. He must be found guilty your—"

Colby interrupted, "Yes, yes, yes, he must be found guilty, but first let's hear from the defense."

Maria began quite logically for a five year-old public defender of grasshoppers, "When you picked him up, he was afraid. He did what any grasshopper would do. He spit on you to make you let him down. He's not guilty!"

"Are you through?" Colby asked impatiently.

Defiantly, Maria asserted, "Yes and he's not guilty!"

This was obviously a trial by judge as you've heard nothing about a jury. And, to any one present, it was obvious what the verdict was going to be because the gallows had been constructed by Colby right before the trial.

I stood and prompted Colby, "The verdict your Honor?"

"Hang'em!" was the reply.

"Noooooo!" cried Maria running toward the house and therefore toward our parents.

Now, I don't really think hanging does much to hurt an insect with a chitinic exoskeleton and no arteries or other vessels for its circulatory system. But, still the little grasshopper looked pitiful as it tried to wriggle free from the thread around its neck.

After an appropriate amount of time, we took the thread off, set the little guy down and, when he hopped away, we headed for Colby's house.

As we entered, we heard Maria's pained voice telling my Mom "I told them he wasn't guilty, but they hanged him anyway!"

She was right, but I pray that little sister never loses that desire to help the oppressed and defend the defenseless. I also pray that she learns that, while boys can be cruel at times (especially when playing roles they've seen in movies), as they mature that soft spot that really does exist in their hearts usually grows and crowds out the cruelty. May she learn these things as clearly as she learned that there was no justice to be found that day in a kangaroo court for a grasshopper.

10
Suicide Bridge

After Colby's folks moved from Uncle John and Aunt Ethel's house to the little white house about 6 miles away, we started using a new swimming hole, dubbed, the bridge. It was named for the big steel and concrete structure that loomed high above the relatively shallow swimming area below—the structure that became known as Suicide Bridge.

Along with Colby's new house came a lot of other new things. There was a new area of woods behind the house, but rather than taking 50 or 60 miles to find signs of civilization, it took less than two miles to realize others were, or had recently been, there.

A more positive development was the new swimming hole. Rather than being two and one-half miles away, like our old swimming hole had been, the bridge was only a half mile from Colby's house. The river was pretty warm but was also pretty shallow and the bottom was almost all rocks. There was very little sand. The beach had some sand but you usually had to move a few rocks to create a nice soft spot for your towel.

The bridge above the river was part of the Redwood Highway. It was heavily traveled by tourists in the summer, but they couldn't really see us swimming much unless we went way up or down river, because the swimming hole was almost directly under the bridge.

As we swam, Colby and I couldn't help but look high above to the top of the concrete guardrails lining the bridge and wonder, "Could a person actually survive, uninjured if they jumped from that bridge?"

Well I measured the water depth where you would most likely make impact. It was about 7 feet 1 inch deep. The bottom was nearly all oval-shaped rocks worn smooth from years of abrasion from dirt, sand, and rock. I also estimated the height of the top of the bridge rail above the water. It was just over 40 feet.

Now I had jumped from as high as 50 feet, from the old railroad bridge on the Rogue River in Grants Pass. There you even had to jump out about 10 feet to clear the rocks. But the water depth was about 15 feet, so you didn't need to worry about the impact with the bottom. I suppose you could let yourself touch bottom, but it would be a very soft touch and one that you chose to make, not one that was forced upon you.

To be sure, the bridge called out to Colby and me. We could hear it taunting, "Jump, you cowards, jump! You know you can't resist for ever, so just jump now and get it over with."

Whenever thoughts of jumping really started invading our minds, two concerns entered our thinking that repeatedly stopped us in our tracks. First, we knew of no one, kid or adult, who had ever jumped from the bridge. That ought to have told us something right there. Second, seven feet one inch of water overlaying a bit of rocks just didn't seem enough to ensure that something bad would not happen to anyone who made the leap. It just looked like a suicide bridge, so that's what we called it.

Now calling it a suicide bridge did not stop the bridge from calling to us, "Jump, you two, it will all be OK. You just need to make that first jump, you chickens!"

Colby and I decided to do something about our dilemma. As we surveyed the water and the bridge we came up with a plan. Colby's part was to exhaustively search the Illinois Valley for anyone who had jumped from the bridge or anyone who knew someone who had jumped. If he found someone who had jumped, he was to get the details of any injuries, death, *etc.* and enter that into our body of bridge knowledge. I was to use my meager knowledge of physics to calculate our downward velocity at impact and to get enough information to see what our impact velocity on the river bottom would be after penetrating seven feet one inch of water.

Without even doing any calculations, I already knew we would still be moving at a good clip when we hit the bottom, I could verify that by jumping far out from our school's high dive into the area that was only eight feet deep. Sure enough, I hit bottom, not too hard, but considering that our high dive was only 15 feet and the bridge at least 40 feet, I was worried. So I started to work on the physics. First I simplified the calculation a lot by just using the acceleration of gravity and neglecting all of the other terms in the equation of motion.

I told Colby, "I'm not 100 percent sure, but I think we'll hit the water at a little under 50 miles per hour. What happens next depends upon how fast we can put on the brakes."

"What if we just did a big cannonball?" Colby queried.

"You know the natural split in your rear end? Well you would probably get split into two pieces starting right there," I quipped. "The best thing we can do is to enter the water like an arrow, so we don't split ourselves open, and figure out some way to slow down as soon as we enter the water."

Colby came right back with the question that pretty well summed up the dilemma, "If we enter like an arrow, toes pointed, hands over our heads, we are almost seven feet long. Whatcha' gonna' do before you go one more inch that's gonna actually slow you down?"

"Just let me think. I'm working on something," was my reply. You see the reason we were doing all this thinking about my calculations was because Colby couldn't find one smidgen of evidence that anyone had ever jumped from that bridge. While I was still thinking, Colby started swimming across the river. I followed. As soon as he hit the far side of the river he started crawling up the steep bank created from the fill dirt and rock that was used to support one end of the ridge. I scampered up the bank after him.

In a couple minutes there stood two boys on the bridge rail (nearly a foot wide) suspiciously eyeing the water far below. We surveyed the bottom of the river which was visible in amazing detail through the clear water.

"See that patch of sand on the bottom," Colby asked me with growing confidence in his voice.

"Yeah, I see it. It must be all of three inches in diameter," I said sarcastically.

Actually it was about three feet across and, if we could be assured of hitting it, we might avoid any injury to our feet or legs. Colby just stared at it for about 10 minutes from our position on the bridge railing. I really didn't know what was going through his mind. I was afraid to ask and I was afraid not to. I really was afraid he was preparing to jump. That scared me a lot because I knew that then I would also have to leap before he hit the water. It was the unspoken code of boyhood honor. I would have been known as "chicken guts" at least until I turned 21 if I didn't jump with him. Now that really posed a problem, because a three-foot circle of sand was at most big enough for one lucky boy to hit. If that's what Colby jumped for, I was left with nothin' but rocks.

Finally Colby turned and started walking down the bridge railing to the far end and I started to breathe again. We climbed down the bank and swam back across the river. No further mention of the bridge was made for the rest of the day by either Colby or me.

The next day broke sunny and warm but grew downright hot by midmorning. So, right after lunch we found ourselves back at the bridge swimming hole. This time I broached the subject first, "I've been thinking about how to jump into shallow water and I think I've got a solution that will work for any situation where the water is a little deeper than we are tall."

"So you figured out how to stop in one inch, huh?" Colby said continuing the sarcasm I had begun using the day before.

This bridge thing was beginning to test our relationship. Seeing that we needed to resolve the Suicide Bridge issue soon, I replied, "We need to start slowing down our speed the first instant we hit the water—we can't wait until our whole body is under water."

"Then how are we gonna do that straight-as-an-arrow thing to keep from splitting our buns in two?"

"Here's my idea," I explained. "As our pointed toes just enter the water, we just pull our toes up by rotating our feet like when you're trying to touch your toes. By the time we get that done we'll be at least in the water up to our waists. So then we just relax and bend at the waist. Got the picture yet?"

"Yeah, we get bent up like a pretzel so they don't need a full-size coffin to bury us in," Colby said sharply.

"No, we'll just do the world's fastest U'y. Our feet will end up near the top of the water and our heads will be down near the bottom. If I'm right, our backs will bottom out just above the river bottom. We'll pull a few G's during the U'y but we shouldn't even touch bottom and won't get hurt at all," I said with more assurance than I felt.

"What happens if we're a little slow in the execution?"

"We'll probably scrape our backs on the bottom a little."

"Or break our backs on the bottom," Colby spit out as he jumped in the river and swam for the other side.

"Here we go again," I thought as I jumped in after him.

A couple of minutes later we both were standing on the bridge rail above the middle of the river just like yesterday. I could tell Colby wanted to jump because he struck the pose where you crouch down with your hands out in front of you. Heck, I wanted to jump too, but fear of the unknown held me back. The fame of being the first to jump from Suicide Bridge just wasn't enough enticement.

Just then Colby leaped straight for the patch of sand. Now that was more than enough enticement—it was coercion! So I jumped before he was hardly off from the bridge rail. As we fell toward the water there was no, "Geronimoooo!" There was only silence, until the wind began to roar in my ears from my fall rate.

Just as Colby accidentally missed the patch of sand to the right, I missed it on purpose a little to the left and thought, "At least 50 miles per hour!" as I hit the water.

Then my toes hit something hard. But, the hard thing was also very slippery because it was covered with slimy river-bottom moss. So my feet sort of ricocheted smoothly off the rock I had hit and caused me to stub my toe a bit on an adjacent rock. It smarted some but any pain was completely lost in the wild rush of exhilaration coursing through my entire mind and body. We had survived a jump from Suicide Bridge! Not only survived, but as soon as Colby and I broke the surface, we were already pulling hard for the far side of the river. We then scampered up the bank, ran out on the bridge railing, and jumped again. This cycle was repeated until we were too exhausted to climb the steep bank even one more time, so we just lay in the sand by the river and relished every moment of that glorious afternoon.

Colby and I made countless jumps on the many subsequent visits to Suicide Bridge. They were not all without injury. My first miscue came on the very next visit after our initial jump. I wanted to do that U'y thing, so I wouldn't have to worry about where I hit the bottom. I got the basics all down first, in like an arrow second, rotate toes and feet upon entry, and third, bend at the waist.

I was a wee bit slow on that "bend at the waist" part. I did the U'y, but my back drug on the rocks at the bottom giving me a nasty little abrasion on my lower back.

When Colby and I started jumping just as cars passed on the highway—trying to make it look like we were falling unintentionally—that's when some more injuries occurred. After feigning one fall, Colby could not regain his balance; as a result, he was not vertical when he reached the water—he was leaning to his right side. Well, his right side, from under his arm to the bottom of his rib cage, was one huge red welt.

While trying to pull the same stunt, I hit the water with my right elbow out a few inches from my body and bent at about a 30-degree angle. I got a nice red welt from my armpit to my elbow.

I should've known to be more careful because I had prior educational experience with bad water landings. You see in my PE class, every Friday the guys and the girls all got to use the pool together. This inevitably led to a bunch of guys trying to do goofy things from the high dive to impress the girls. My contribution was a dive I invented called the airplane dive. It has only been performed once from the high dive, to the best of my knowledge—by me. There's a reason for that. All you have to do to perform this dive is take a big bounce and then start a swan dive with your arms outstretched to either side. That's where you leave them—out like airplane wings as you hit the water. The main drawbacks to this dive are that the water smacks your head like a two-by-four and then rips your arms down like you're trying to clap your hands a foot or so behind the small of your back. The effect is amazingly painful—both shoulders are nearly dislocated. Now I had pretty good upper body strength in those days. Without it I probably would have dislocated both shoulders.

At the bridge, I had forgotten the lesson of the airplane dive and consequently received a painful welt and a sore shoulder to remind me. That injury was deserved. But the other injury I got, our next time at the bridge, just wasn't fair. I had no idea what was coming and it took me a while to realize what had happened.

On one of my routine jumps from the bridge, I jumped the gun a bit with rotating my feet while doing the U'y. My right foot came up nearly parallel with the water a split-second before I hit, which was also a split-second before I split the bottom of my big toe wide open. Since my foot hit sort of flat, my big toe entered the water with that smacking sound that a beaver's tail makes. After the splat, since the U'y wasn't executed properly, both feet plowed into the bottom and buried into the small patch of sand. When I came up, my right toe went from being almost numb to really stinging with enough intensity that I swam to shore to have a look.

What I saw was a cut down the middle of my toe that looked like somebody had slit it with a razor blade. Since I hit the sand on the bottom, the cut was further irritated by being full of sand. I couldn't believe that the water which had been my friend and given me so much delight could turn on me and slit me open like a box cutter slits a cardboard box. Well, I soon figured out that skin which hits the water flat from that height gets split. I hollered and complained about it until Colby went through our stuff and found a band-aid which I wrapped tightly around my split toe so I could continue jumping.

When we finally learned to properly respect the height we were jumping from, the injuries ceased. Then there was nothing left but sheer exhilarating fun.

One weekend it really got fun! That was when Colby's Uncle Garth and his family flew in to the little smoke jumper's airport near O'Brien in Garth's four-passenger plane. One of the things that Garth packed into the plane for the trip was his movie camera.

It got really hot that afternoon, so everybody jumped in cars, except Colby and I who jumped on our Honda's, and we all headed for the bridge. Garth brought along his movie camera. When he saw what Colby and I were doing (standing on the bridge rail) he started the camera rolling. With both our moms screaming because they had never seen us jump before (mostly because we hadn't bothered telling them about jumping prior to this—you know, with parents ignorance is bliss) we performed every kind of jump we knew including our synchronized side-by-side jump. Garth got it all on film which he rushed down to get developed. Before uncle Garth flew back home, we had watched our jumps countless times. When Garth reversed the projector, everyone roared with laughter as Colby and I exploded from the water and leaped backward clear up to the bridge railing. We all must've watched those scenes 50 times, both forward and backward.

So, at last, the scary unknown of Suicide Bridge had become a place we knew intimately, and a place that gave us jillions of joy-filled jumps. I suppose we were lucky, or protected by our guardian angel, to have learned to jump safely with only a few minor injuries. For any kids who may be reading this story, before you jump or dive into any water from any height, search for any hidden dangers and learn to jump safely or your bridge may, for an appropriate reason, become known as Suicide Bridge.

The Saltpetre Sagas

The druggist, when he saw Colby and me, chuckled and asked, "Is your Mom making jerky again?"

"Yep. How'd you know?" asked Colby feigning surprise.

"Because it seems that every time I see you two here you're coming to buy some saltpetre."

Saltpetre, also known as potassium nitrate, was really that easy to buy in the 50's. Just tell the man that your Mom is making jerky, drying fish or making pickles. Actually you didn't even have to tell him why you wanted it. Saltpetre was for sale for anyone with enough money to buy it and it was cheap.

Now you might wonder why Colby and I would want saltpetre of all things. After all, it's just some chemical used to mess up men's masculinity, right? Wrong! Let's clear up a few common misconceptions here. First, saltpetre is NOT used in military basic training or in prisons and it does NOT do what it is rumored to do.

Okay, with that settled, here's a free chemistry tip for the non-chemically inclined. Whenever you hear a chemical compound named potassium "something-or-other," think explode or burn, because potassium is really good at both of those things.

Ever since Colby's Dad had let it slip that potassium nitrate mixed with something for it to oxidize could be used to make gunpowder, Colby and I had been buying canisters of the stuff like crazy (which at times we were).

It didn't take long for us to find that the energy stored in sugar oxidizes wonderfully if you use a little saltpetre to set it off. So Colby and I began our experiments to determine the best saltpetre-sugar ratios to use for a wide range of pyrotechnical applications. And, so began the three stories I have called, "The Saltpetre Sagas."

11
The Angry Bee

"Did you see that?" Colby asked with an excitement tinged voice reserved for our moments of great discovery.

"Yeah, it burned hot, fast, and completely," I responded with more than a little interest.

"Mom was just about out of sugar, so I just put in all she had. Didn't think we had enough for this batch to do much."

"Maybe that's the trick—less sugar and you get a faster, cleaner burn," I hypothesized.

Colby had "borrowed" all the sugar in his Mom's sugar jar, but it wasn't as much as we thought we needed. Consequently we ended up with a lean mix of sugar with saltpetre and, in the process, stumbled upon a formula for making a powerful rocket fuel, or perhaps an angry bee.

Now Colby and I had long dreamed of making our own rocket, not just the rocket's structure, but the whole thing including the fuel—you know, like NASA. They can't just build some metal shell then run to the hobby store to buy Jetex fuel (used for manufactured rocket kits). They have to build the whole thing themselves, rocket, engine and fuel. That's what Colby and I wanted to do, build that whole sucker from scratch, thus proving our engineering expertise.

Years earlier we had discovered that you can make a mini-rocket with a 22 caliber rifle bullet. Twenty-two shorts worked best because the casing was lighter. Now when you fire a 22 the firing pin pushes really hard on the cap which pops, exploding inward to ignite the gunpowder inside of the shell which, in turn, makes the bullet head fly out of the shell and out of the barrel of the gun.

Now most of you know about that sequence. But Colby and I reversed most of that sequence to create our mini-rocket. For example, you first pull the bullet head out of the shell, then you lay the shell rear-end up on some kind of a ramp which makes a trail of gunpowder leak out of the casing. You light the gunpowder and it burns backwards to the cap making it explode backward into the shell and, due to Newton's third law of motion (for every action there is an equal and opposite reaction), the shell casing turns into a brass mini-rocket, and flies about thirty feet in the opposite direction that the bullet would have traveled. You see it don't you? Just reverse the firing process of a bullet and, *voila*, a mini-rocket.

The only thing wrong with the mini-rocket is that there's very little satisfaction left after you discover that this works and then launch two or three shell casings into the lower atmosphere. You have no input into the design—that's built into bullets. You just get a ready-made rocket that's not even aerodynamic and to which you can't add any fuel for a longer flight, or do any other fun things with it for that matter. You just pull, light, pop and then it's over.

To create something more satisfying, Colby and I sat down in his Dad's shop to design our own rocket using materials we could come up with around Colby's place. We already had created the fuel. We just needed to concentrate on the rocket and its engine.

It was clear that the fuselage needed to be a durable, lightweight tube. As we sat in the shop brainstorming our rocket's design my eyes came to rest upon Colby's BB gun on the nearby workbench. Beside the gun sat a large package of BBs. Now we grew up in the days of Red Ryder and other Daisy BB guns. Ammunition for these air rifles was in abundant supply. You could get anything from a small tube with a few hundred BBs to a large six-inch tube holding thousands. My eyes were fixed on the large tube variety and it looked to be about one inch in diameter.

I was already calculating how many ounces of fuel we could pack into that cylinder of glue-hardened paper as I verbalized my idea to Colby, "Hey, if we use the big BB pack, and if we can find a way to restrict the exhaust coming out of the tube, we've got ourselves a rocket body and an engine. Bet it would fly for a minute or more depending on the size of the hole on the back end."

Colby congratulated me with, "Good idea!" Then from out of nowhere he pulled a one-inch diameter, light weight plastic washer. "Glue this on the back end and we've got our jet engine."

"Great idea! But it's really hard to guess how big the opening needs to be for a good flight," I added.

Now we both knew that if the orifice was too big the fuel would burn in one big explosion and our rocket wouldn't fly any higher or farther than our little 22 shell casings—that is, if the rocket even survived the initial explosion. If on the other hand, the hole was too small, the burn would be too slow with too little thrust and all we would have created is a roman candle lying on its side shooting out orange flames. That wouldn't be any fun—

we could buy a roman candle at the fireworks stand for less than the cost of a canister of saltpetre. Then there was the possibility that if the orifice was way too small we would just have a big firecracker that would surely blow our rocket to smithereens.

We needed to get that orifice sized right or all was for naught. The problem was we weren't sophisticated enough to calculate the size of the orifice up front. We had to find the right size empirically, by trial and possibly error. The risk of this was large enough that we scrapped our plans for a manned space flight, so Colby turned the grasshopper astronaut loose, being careful not to let it spit tobacco juice on him.

I'm sure you know that if that orifice was sized right there probably wouldn't be much of a story to tell. So, yes, we got it all wrong. But, how we erred and what happened as a result is what makes this story so bizarre and hopefully entertaining. For Colby and me, the rest of the story, though educational, it was not entertaining. But, let's get back to the rocket construction.

Colby found some thin balsa that we cut the tail fins out of. So we just needed to finish the head of the rocket. I reached into my pocket and pulled out just what we needed.

You see, my house was next to the local golf course. Only an unused field separated my parent's property from part of one fairway that lay some 40 or 50 yards from the men's tee. Any ball hit off from the toe of the driver was sure to wind up in the field, which was overgrown with weeds and tall grass. I found a lot of golf balls there.

The women's tee was right next to the field—only a wire fence lay in between. A lot of tees ended up by the fence where I could reach through the wire and grab them.

Colby and I always had an ample supply of golf balls and tees. The things we did with these fifties-vintage golf balls (which are each wrapped in a million miles of rubber bands) is another story for another time.

Where were we—let's see—I had pulled a blue golf tee out of my pocket and Colby thought it would make a dandy nose for our rocket. The sharp end of the tee would be sure to punish anything that the rocket flew into.

With copious globs of glue and a little duct tape we assembled our pointy-nosed rocket which we named the "model tee" rocket for several obvious reasons. After a few hours of glue-drying time, Colby began cramming our rocket fuel blend of saltpetre and sugar through the hole in the washer and into the BB-package tube that would soon contain the inferno which would blast our rocket into the wild blue yonder.

Next, we sawed off a square piece of a two-by-ten board to use as our launching pad. Then Colby went into his room and came back with a coil of fuse material—the kind you get when you buy Jetex pellets for model rockets. The fuse was our only concession to commercially available rocket components.

Well, the moment had arrived, so we took the rocket and pad out into the street by Colby's house. The street was actually a five-mile long country road that only had five houses along it. There was seldom any traffic.

In those magical moments of twilight, a time when all things seem possible to a boy, we stood the little rocket on its tail fins on the launching pad with its golf-tee nose pointed up into the sky. As the evening star made its appearance, we counted down from ten and then Colby lit the fuse.

Maybe Colby and I should have made a wish upon that star. Or, maybe we just shouldn't have lit the rocket. But there were no maybe's about one thing; we should have had a course in aeronautical engineering before we built that little demon.

Because, there ain't no way a short, stubby little rocket with a whole lot of power can fly in a straight line for more than say, a thousandth of a second.

To describe what happened next requires me to use two analogies to even attempt to relate the rocket's behavior to you. So, bear with me as I develop them.

The first analogy comes from a model of the atom. Back when I took chemistry we were taught a modified version of the Bohr Theory of atomic structure. To make a long story short, it was thought that electrons orbited the nucleus of the atom at a certain radius—sort of like a planet around the sun. But in three dimensions, an electron would move a long the surface of a sphere that's defined by a constant radius from the nucleus. In a moment I'll reduce the three-dimensional sphere down into a two-dimensional plane—you'll get the picture clear enough when I do that, so just hang with me for a moment.

Upon hearing that electrons moved along the surface of a sphere around the nucleus, I asked my teacher, "How do they move along this sphere? Is it like a planet in orbit?"

The reply I got was quite surprising to me, "They move in a frenzy, as if they are trying to fill the entire orbit all at the same time," the teacher told me. I don't think that explanation was one-hundred percent scientifically accurate, but it pretty well described the movement of our rocket which, by the way, was quite surprising to both Colby and me.

As Colby lit the fuse, we had visions of a trail of fire streaking up into the evening sky as our little rocket broke through the tropopause and flamed out somewhere in the stratosphere high above us. We were dreamers—at least for a second or two before we became screamers. You remember that little orifice size problem I mentioned earlier, well it surfaced about this time.

Colby's washer just had too big a hole in it. Consequently, we got a fast burn with a heck of a lot of flame, but not nearly enough vertical thrust. As a result our little rocket lifted up off the launch pad about three feet then tilted over nearly parallel to the ground. It was tilted up less than five degrees, but that gave it enough upward thrust to keep that flaming viper three feet above the ground. This left most of the rest of the thrust directed in the horizontal direction, so the rocket could move really fast horizontally. The trouble with that was that I could see the tail of that rocket swinging side to side like a pendulum. The swinging motion distributed the horizontal thrust through all of the angles in its plane. To simplify this a bit, the rocket was going to fly all over the place really fast, but only three feet off the ground.

So what Colby and I had was a rocket spewing a big ball of fire out its rear as it tried to fill all of the space three feet above that country toad—a space also occupied by Colby and me. When I ran to my left, the rocket was there. When I ran to my right, it was there too. Colby tried the same random running escape and had the same result I did. That little flame thrower was everywhere all at once with its fiery flatus scorching everything it passed.

Now Colby and I had on cut-off jeans so our bare legs were easy prey. They were thoroughly singed as we got our own personal preview of Hades with each passage of that fire ball, and it seemed that there were an infinite number of scorching passages.

We screamed in pain, jumped, twisted and shouted—years before the Beatles ever recorded that song—even before Phil Spector wrote that doggone ditty. All we saw was that any attempt to dodge that little burning booger was futile.

Now I need that second analogy that I mentioned to continue this story, so bear with me a moment.

Have you ever really aroused the anger of a bumblebee? Well, when I was four somehow I irritated a big bumblebee. When he attacked like a buzz bomber, I swatted at him and tried to run away, but he just seemed to come at me from all angles at once. He terrorized me like that until he latched onto my upper lip and stung it right below one nostril. Of course I yelped and cried from the fiery sting, but the pain was nothing compared to what happened a few minutes later.

Normally I could run barefoot through our clover-covered lawn, step on several honeybees working the clover, get stung on my foot a few times, and it was no big deal. It just stung for a minute and then it was all over. Not so with the bumblebee. One side of my upper lip began to swell and eventually got so big that it plugged the nostril on that side. It was a pitiful sight to see. I looked as if I had grabbed my upper lip and tried to stretch it over my nose.

My aunt and uncle (more like big sister and big brother because they were only four and five years older than me respectively) were there when I swelled up. They started calling me all sorts of clever and cruel names like "balloon lip," "pug mouth," and they said I was "booger-blocked." They even told me I was so hideous that I should run away, join the circus, and become a freak in a side show. The stigma was worse than the sting. That bumblebee really knew how to hurt a boy.

The rocket Colby and I built brought back memories of the bumblebee that had attacked me from every angle all at once. The buzz of the bumblebee and the sizzling sound of the rogue rocket mingled in my mind. But unlike the bumblebee incident, the stinging and the panic from the ferocity of the rocket attack were far worse than the ensuing stigma—the stigma from our failure in our debut as rocketeers.

As our last screams echoed through the evening air, the rocket fell to the road and its fiery flatulence flickered out. Hearts still pounding, legs singed to near hairlessness, and clothes blackened by burns, Colby and I just thanked God that our time of terror had been terminated.

Colby and I swore right then and there that we would never build another rocket until we were sure we could design one that would do more than serve as a visual model of electron motion. We would ever never again place ourselves at the mercy of the angry bee.

12
Meteorites And UFOs

There were times when Colby and I saw things in the night that spooked us. When we grew a bit older, we wanted to share the terror we felt from meteorites and UFOs.

The year was 1956. The place was the drive-in theater in Cave Junction, a few miles from Colby's house. The movie playing was the documentary from United Artists called, UFO. Colby's older sister, A.J., had talked one of her friends into giving Colby and me a ride to the drive-in to see UFO. Of course, little brother could not sit in the car with a big sister and her friends during the movie, so Colby and I sat in the outdoor chairs fairly close to the big screen. We got an IMAX-like view of enough's scenes of UFOs and supposed alien abductions that our young boyish imaginations kept conjuring up visions that scared us to death. The people in the movie who saw UFOs were responsible adults like USAF pilots. People died or disappeared in some cases. Yes, we were scared, but we would never have admitted it—at least not during the movie.

I may have mentioned that Colby's house was about two miles from one end of a small rural road named, Cemetery Road.

There was only one house along that stretch of unlighted country road. The movie didn't end until after midnight. That was when we were informed that Colby's sister's friend would drop us off at the end of the road, but would not take us all the way to Colby's house. What terrible thing to do to your little brother!

What big sister would make her little brother run the gauntlet of alien abductors and other unnamed terrors lurking behind every shadowy form of a bush or tree along Cemetery Road? The answer—a big sister who wasn't scared witless by the movie. Or, more likely, a big sister who doesn't have to walk that road herself. Do you know how many trees and bushes line the sides of two miles of country road?

Finally resigning ourselves to our fate of death, or dissection at the hands of little bald green men, Colby and I started down the dark road at about 12:30 AM. There was no moon that night and, though the stars were bright, they only gave just enough light to create hundreds of dark shadows along our way. Every sensory nerve in our bodies was on high alert—DEFCON 2. Neither of us uttered a sound because our voices might have drowned out the very sound to which we needed to react in order to save our lives. Then, over to our left near that menacing manzanita bush, we heard one of those sounds that sent us to DEFCON 1, and we responded with what we hoped was life-saving action.

Colby broke into a run. At his cue, with over a mile still to go, I broke into an all-out sprint. I don't mean to brag, but I was not just a fast runner—I was like greased lightning. At twelve years of age I ran the 40 in 4.3 seconds, good wide receiver speed in the NFL. Though I was only eleven at this time, my sprinting speed that night was close to what it was going to be next year. The amazing thing was that I kept up the speed for the full distance. I sure wish my track coach could have had a stop watch on me to see the world record for the mile get smoked that night by a bug-eyed eleven year old boy with aliens after him.

Now when adrenaline gives a person such amazing ability, there's a huge debt to be paid at the other end, called oxygen debt. I honestly couldn't tell whether I really needed oxygen or whether I was hyperventilating. It just felt like I couldn't catch my breath. I was still bent over with my hands on my knees making raspy, throaty, gasping noises and feeling like I was suffocating, when Colby trotted up. He was alive and well and there were no aliens on his tail. If I could just catch my breath, it looked like we would come out of this with our bodies and all of our organs intact.

"You OK?" Colby asked, breathing pretty hard himself.

But I still couldn't talk yet, so I just continued the raspy gasping that fell fall far short of sucking in the volume of air that my body was demanding. As my breathing panic subsided, I remember thinking, "I know it must have been a world record, but nobody's ever gonna' know." I felt kind of like the pastor that called in sick one Sunday morning so he could play golf and, when he shot a 60, setting the course record, there was absolutely no satisfaction from his achievement because there was no one he could tell.

Colby and I never talked specifically about the night we made that run for our lives or the fears that prompted it. But we remembered every terror-stricken nanosecond of it. Those memories were to haunt us again, later that summer.

One hot summer night a month, or so later, Colby and I thought sleeping outside where it cooled off more quickly sounded like a good idea. Outside it got at least 10 degrees cooler than inside the house. We grabbed our sleeping bags, a rope from the shop, and then headed into the woods behind Colby's house. We made camp, being sure to place the rope on the ground so it completely encircled both of our sleeping bags.

Colby's Dad had told stories about hunters waking up with rattlesnakes in their sleeping bags. They couldn't move a muscle until the snake crawled out, possibly right by their faces as it rattled a bit and exited the sleeping bag after the sun came up the next day. Colby's Dad also told us the old woodsman's tale that a snake would not cross a rope on the ground even for the warm sanctuary of a person's sleeping bag.

As the veracity of the tale was being debated by Colby and me, something above caught our eyes and we looked up. While sometimes I may use hyperbole for affect when telling stories about Colby, this is no exaggeration—we saw a meteorite that created a larger and brighter light in the sky than a full moon. It fell somewhere to the east of us leaving a tail that covered half of the sky. The big orange ball of fire had a black hole inside its circumference. That really looked weird. Also, the meteorite appeared to hit the earth very close to us, about two miles to the east, just beyond the ridge line behind Colby's property.

My mind immediately began calculating how long it might take a little bald green man to walk two miles. But then I wondered, "What if the alien had something to help him move faster than just a walk?"

Well evidently Colby was doing the same calculations and coming to the same conclusions as me—the alien arrival was imminent.

Our eyes met. No words were exchanged—none were necessary. We both stood, rolled up our sleeping bags, and trotted back to the house. We slept on Colby's feather mattress and did not feel like playing duck-down tickle torture that night. Fear had already tortured us enough.

Later, Colby and I talked about the large meteorite and we scanned the newspapers for a couple of days until we found an article about it. Scientists were looking for it, but we never heard that was found.

We never did mention the aliens in any of our conversations. The meteorite, however, created such an impression on us, and such a stir in the community, that we never forgot it. A few years later we tried to recreate the meteorite incident, but that was after Colby made his discovery—when he found that the melting point of both sugar and saltpetre is a few degrees lower than the flash point of their mixture.

Colby's Dad kept a hot plate on one of the benches in his shop right next to the old anvil Judge Colby used to hit with his gavel to bring the court to order. I never did see him use it for anything, but Colby soon got the idea that we might be able to better package our saltpetre bombs and fuel if we melted the mixture and molded it into the desired shape, then let it cool and harden.

In order to test the hypothesis about melting and molding our mixture it was necessary that we test it by very, very slowly heating some of the mixture up in a pan on the hot plate. I stood across the room as Colby gently nudged the temperature control up every 30 seconds or so. If we were wrong, the best-case scenario would be that a smoke bomb would go off in Colby's face. The worst-case would be that there would be an explosion that injured Colby and burned down his Dad's shop.

I prayed, held my breath, hugged the wall on the other side of the room more tightly, and kept one eye on the hot plate and the other on the door, my only escape route.

In recent years this might have played out differently. Today, a couple of boys could just look up the melting points and flashpoints of the compounds on the internet and use a thermometer to attempt this in a much safer manner. But, I have a feeling that even if we had been born in the 1990's, Colby would still have preferred to do this seat-of-the-pants. That's just the way Colby was.

After treading ever so lightly through a heating process that lasted about 20 minutes, the crystalline mixture started melting. Colby stopped turning up the heat and watched that melting process.

What happened next caught me entirely by surprise. I thought Colby had really lost it when he reached into the pan with a bare hand. He scooped out a clump of the molten potassium nitrate and sugar, quickly rolled it into a ball and pinched it to produce a nub that protruded a quarter of an inch or so from the little ball. By then the molten stuff had returned to a solid state.

I hadn't realized it (but evidently Colby had) that despite 20 minutes of heating, the pan still wasn't hot enough to burn your fingers as long as you moved them quickly. As that realization dawned on me, so did the realization of what Colby had just fashioned. He had made a cute little round firebomb with a nub to use as a fuse. I started enumerating the things we could do with it.

Well we took the cute little guy outside and lit the nub with a match. There was only a very small fraction of a second between the lighting of the nub and the fiery blast created by the little round firebomb. Watching the molded ball of saltpetre and sugar ignite and burn gave me an idea.

My chemistry teacher had taught earlier in the year that you can usually increase the rate of oxidation by increasing the amount of oxygen the oxidant is exposed to. What better way of doing that, I thought, then to get the ball of molded saltpetre and sugar moving rapidly through the air.

Now, a neighbor down the road from my house, Howard P, had taught me quite by accident that, if you move something that's on fire rapidly through the air, man it really burns! Howard was about 10 years older than me. He and his Dad operated a dairy just down the road from my house. Howard loved a good joke, but on the day I was thinking about, the joke was on Howard. He had just bought himself a small motorcycle and was trying it out by running it up and down the highway in front of my house. He stopped right across the road from my house to check something on the bike, then lit a cigarette (Howard smoked in his earlier days). Then he hopped on the bike and gunned it. I watched as the cigarette began to glow bright red on the tip. Then, as Howard hit about 40 miles-per-hour, the little red ember burst into a big ball of flame that coalesced with Howard's head. Howard braked rapidly to a stop, spitting out the flaming cigarette, stomping on what was left, and checking his singed eyebrows, eyelashes, and hair. It was pretty funny, especially since Howard wasn't hurt seriously. It was also pretty impressive that the little cigarette could turn into a foot-wide ball of flame just by putting it in a 40 mile-per-hour breeze.

Well, I told Colby my idea of what we should do with molded balls of saltpetre and sugar. He bought in immediately, so we headed for the hardware store where we bought 10 feet of surgical rubber tubing. When we got back to Colby's place, I started to work on the super slingshot we would need while Colby began melting the rocket fuel mixture of saltpetre and sugar on the hot plate and molding a whole bunch of 1 1/2 inch diameter balls of rocket fuel.

I carefully measured my arm span—just over five feet from the palm on one hand to my thumb tip on the other. Then I cut two lengths of surgical rubber tubing that would just barely stretch to that length. I completed my slingshot by tying the rubber pieces firmly onto both sides of a slingshot handle I had cut from a madrone tree and then adding a pouch made from the tongue of an old leather shoe on the other end of the two pieces of tubing.

By that time Colby had made eight or nine balls of fuel each with a little nub, I had just built the most powerful slingshot I could possibly pull. Colby told Larry R, a neighbor boy, what we were up to when he dropped in unexpectedly and then we waited for darkness. Actually, I began some preliminary testing while it was still daylight. I shot a few round rocks about the size of the balls of saltpetre and sugar that Colby had made. The slingshot's power was very impressive! Most of the rocks just disappeared into the air, they were moving too fast for our eyes to track. By repeatedly shooting toward a nearby lake as we backed away from it, we determined that the slingshot could easily shoot a rock 300 yards.

Well the twilight faded and darkness finally arrived. So did Larry—he wasn't about to miss this.

Colby handed me a ball of saltpetre and sugar, I placed it in the slingshot pouch leaving the nub exposed on top and drew the rubber all the way back, angling the shot up into the air. Colby struck a match and passed the flame by the little nub fuse. As soon as I saw ignition, I let her fly!

"Great balls of fire!" yelled Larry as the little ball became a huge ball of fire ten feet or more in diameter and made a whooshing sound until it reached three hundred feet or so where it disappeared as all the fuel was consumed. Nothing floated back down at all—no embers—nothing! This meant we could shoot these burning boogers up wherever we wanted (except into a tree) and there would be no danger of starting a fire—only great balls of fire in the sky.

Simultaneously, Colby and I voiced, "Meteorite." Our huge fireball looked similar, but even more impressive, than the meteorite we had seen, especially if you were within a couple of hundred yards of its path.

I pondered out loud, "Where can we shoot this thing so people will see it?"

Then Colby suggested, but with the tone of a command, "Let's go down to the drive-in."

Well, we all knew what his plan was after he said that. So we grabbed our stuff, hopped on our motorcycles and rode the short distance to Cave Junction's drive-in theater on Redwood Highway.

It was midway through the movie when, from behind the big screen, we fired our meteorite up and over the movie screen—also over the tops of the people in their cars. Surely they had to see that huge fireball flying over the screen and then passing out of sight as it flew over their heads. Some started honking indicating that it had been seen. Whether the honking indicated their pleasure, alarm, or complaint, we didn't know. So, just for good measure, we gave them another big meteorite to think about and then we slunk away under the cover of darkness.

Over the next few days Colby, Larry and I read the papers and listened to the news. Though we had created "great balls of fire," evidently we failed to create anything newsworthy about meteorites and UFOs.

13
Smoked Pig

Our saltpetre sagas began with some trials and some errors as we experimented with different formulas, different oxidants, and different ratios of saltpetre to oxidant. Well, our errors sometimes became trials for other creatures, like when we ended up with a smoked pig.

Colby's Dad would frequently raise his own steer or hog to provide an economical source of meat for his family. Since he worked on the planer at a big lumber mill, he could get for free nearly all the lumber he might need for fences and pens. One day he built a small building that looked to Colby and me a lot like a very large doghouse. It was built up a good 18 inches off from the ground, so Colby's Dad ran a long, heavy plank from the front door down to the ground making a ramp. Then all around the little house he built a six-foot high fence and hung a gate on hinges and secured the newly built pen by adding a latch to the gate.

The next day he brought home a small pig and instructed Colby in his duties regarding the pig's care—care that would turn the little pig into a big hog which Colby's Dad would then turn into smoked ham, ribs, bacon, pork roast, and sausage.

Colby and I soon learned that the little pig loved for you to scratch his side. If we really gave him a good scratching, he would just plop down on his opposite side. As this pig began acting like one, his pen became a real, well, a real pigpen. The mud got to be several inches deep. It became obvious why Colby's Dad had built the little house 18 inches high with the ramp up to the door. The pig needed some time without his cloven feet buried 4 inches deep in the mud where they might become diseased.

We thought it was great fun to coax the pig about two-thirds of the way up the plank and then to scratch his side. When he leaned over to plop onto his other side, man did he plop! The mud splattered everywhere as the little pig fell a foot or so and landed in the muck and mire below. As he grew into a big hog, he could really plop into the mud. We had to stop that little game eventually because we got splattered with almost as much mud as the pig when 300 pounds of pork pounded the muddy ooze.

Before the little guy got that big, one day he developed a balance problem. You see out by the Chinamen's diggings near Takilma (you can read about them in another story), there was an abandoned ranch with an abandoned orchard. Toward the end of summer Colby's family would go and pick apples from the orchard for canning. Now the apples weren't the best and juiciest apples because the orchard hadn't been attended properly for probably fifty years. But the apples were great for pies and apple sauce, so Colby's Mom canned them for such purposes.

The summer of the pig, we really picked a lot of apples. Colby's Mom canned apples and canned apples until she was really tired of canning apples. All of the uncanned apples were set out in a big old galvanized tub. There they lay until they were no longer fit to can. That was when Colby's Mom told Colby and me to feed the old apples to the pig. She didn't tell us how to feed the pig, so Colby grabbed one handle on the old tub and I grabbed the other handle. We carried the tub to the pigpen and dumped all 30 pounds or so of apples into his feeding trough.

Well, being a pig, the little hog pigged out on apples. The problem was the apples were well into the fermentation process.

When Colby and I returned to the house with the empty tub his Mom asked in disbelief, "You boys didn't feed all those apples to the pig at once, did you?"

"We sure did—why not? He's a pig!" Colby piped up.

"You two had better go check on the pig and take any apples that are left away from him," Colby's Mom instructed.

Obediently, but after dilly dallying for awhile, Colby and I walked out behind the woodshed where the pig pen was and immediately saw that the little guy had eaten every last apple. We heard a strange grunting "oink" and then around one corner of the little pig house waddled a drunken pig. He made a belching noise and fell over into the muck just like when we scratched him on his side. He got to his feet, staggered a few steps, and fell again.

By the next day he had sobered up and lived a largely uneventful pig's life for a couple of weeks. But the little guy's peace was soon to be broken when Colby and I began testing sugar with the saltpetre that we had recently purchased.

Our initial test was a very small-scale experiment where Colby took a pinch of saltpetre and about ten pinches of sugar, mixed them well, poured the mixture onto a small piece of wax paper, twisted it up until it looked like a small bomb, and lit it out in the yard.

Though there wasn't much to burn, it generated an incredible amount of smoke. We realized that this could be the formula for a smoke bomb. So Colby scaled the experiment up a bit.

We wanted to know two things, first, if we scaled our experiment up by about a factor of ten could we generate ten times as much smoke as we had just seen and second, what would be the effects on a person if they were exposed to all that smoke. Colby and I had both heard that, because they responded to many things much like human beings, pigs were often used in research. We both knew what we had to do to scale up the experiment.

Using a big piece of wax paper as the container, we placed two ounces of saltpetre and twenty ounces of sugar on it, mixed them up, and twisted the wax paper up so it looked like a bomb. Then we made a beeline for the pigpen.

With a little scratching and miscellaneous coaxing we got the test specimen up the plank and into the little house (our test facility). Colby pushed the subject into the interior corner of the facility, set the bomb in the center of the floor, lit it, then we ran like heck because we needed clear eyes to observe everything that was about to happen—we couldn't afford to get all smoked up.

Here's what we saw:

Observation number one: Black smoke boiled out of the pig house door like you wouldn't believe (now there's an objective scientific observation)

Observation number two: A terrified pig ran squealing out of the door and, in all of the smoke, missed the plank and fell into the mud below.

The pig was OK now since he was out of the smoke and back home in his element, the muck and mire. But black smoke continued to roll out of the pig house door as the tiny bit of saltpetre tried its best to oxidize all of the sugar, but only succeeded in making smoke—smoke that had resulted in a smoked pig.

14
Two Grizzled Old Men

One Sunday afternoon in late winter Colby and I were trying to do something that we tried at least 30 or 40 times a year, that is to convince Colby's Dad there was so much trash to burn that we needed to build a bonfire to burn it all. We were very effective at convincing him 'cause we would scour the entire property looking for anything that looked like it needed to be burned, put it all in a pile, show the pile to Colby's Dad, and then pop the question.

Our batting average on fires was about 800, so we built a lot of fires over the course of a year. Mostly we did this because Colby liked to play with fire—figuratively as well as literally.

This particular Sunday came near the end of a week of beautiful, mild, sunny weather. Our parents had planned to go visit some friends for the afternoon, but since most everything was still wet, or at least damp from winter, Colby's Dad reasoned that it was safe to leave Colby and me there with our bonfire. He reasoned wrongly!

Well we had gotten the okay to build our fire that day, so we went to work getting the fire going so that we could get down to the real business—playing. Colby and I had several games that we had created. One game was called pop the jar. If I remember correctly, I thought of this game after hearing about Boyle's gas laws in science class. But the thing is, for me it was only a theoretical concept, but for Colby it had to be made to happen in the real world.

The game, pop the jar, went something like this. Wait until the fire burns down and has a huge bed of red hot coals; then get a jar of heavy glass—one that you could seal tightly. Mason jars with lids worked great. Next, you fill the jar about two-thirds with water, screw the lid on really tight, and place the jar gently in the hot coals making sure that the jar is visible from 20 or 30 feet away. Then you wait for Boyle's laws to pop the jar and blow glass shrapnel all over the county.

Colby and I would sit by the fire watching the jar closely. By this time, we had already each located our own oak trees some 20 to 30 feet from the fire. You needed to make sure the trunk of your selected oak tree was bigger around than you were. We waited until we saw the first signs of boiling inside the jar, usually there were a few bubbles. At the boiling point, we would run for our oak trees and put 12 inches or so of solid oak between our bodies and the fire.

What usually transpired next was that we spent two to three minutes sheltered by our own oak tree after which there was a big explosion. Then you would hear the vegetation getting splattered by bits of glass.

That was pop the jar. Oh, I forgot the last part. You see the fire usually got blown apart too, so you had to go beat or stamp out the scattered coals and put pieces of burning wood back on the fire. This last part is why we didn't play pop the jar in the summer. That might have burned up all of southwestern Oregon and besides we had other ways of doing that, like for instance another game we played called, firebug.

Colby invented firebug quite by accident. In our boyhood days, there were still car tires around that required inner tubes. When the tubes got old and too bad to patch anymore—too bad even for floating in the river—we burned them. Their smoke smelled horrible and burned our eyes. So one day Colby pulled a burning inner tube off from the fire to quell the smoke. He grabbed it by the part that hadn't caught on fire yet and drug it across the ground away from the fire. To our surprise, as Colby drug the burning inner tube along, melted globules of molten burning rubber were deposited in the wake of the inner tube. Colby stopped and studied the sight of tiny fires strewn along the inner tube's path. I saw that look in his eyes—wheels were turning in his head and, *voila*, firebug was born.

You can imagine what would happen if you drug the inner tube across a field of dry grass, can't you? I'll bet you're beginning to get a clear picture of this game about now and you're realizing why Colby, the pyromaniac, loved it so much.

Here's how firebug is played. One of us is declared to be the firebug. The other person is the fireman. Somehow I can never remember getting to be the firebug. Colby loved that role so much that I didn't have the heart to demand my rights as he reached for the inner tube each time we played.

The firebug would grab the burning inner tube and run quickly through the field of dry grass near where we built our bonfires. As he ran, the tube left a trail of molten rubber globs. Each glob would very quickly burst into a small grass fire.

The fireman picked up a tree branch before the firebug began his run and trailed along behind the firebug trying to beat out each little fire before it could become a big fire. You can probably see several fatal flaws in the design of this game. On this particular day one of those flaws was very nearly fatal.

In the '50s you could find two kinds of inner tubes, black rubber and red rubber. Most tubes were black rubber. It wasn't as stretchy (not very good for making slingshots) and it didn't burn as well, or make as many fire starting globules as red rubber did.

Red rubber, on the other hand, was stretchy (great for making powerful slingshots) and burned like crazy, pouring out its red rubber globules like red hot lava from a spewing volcano. It was almost as effective as lava at starting fires.

If you'll remember I said that this story takes place after two weeks of unusually mild, sunny weather in late winter. Let me explain why that is important. During the summer, grasses and weeds grow to about 18 inches high in that field. As summer ends, the vegetation dries making the field look a bit like a wheat field at harvest time. During the winter two things take place. First, the rain and snow knock down part (about half) of the dry vegetation. Second, new green grass grows up from the ground to three or four inches high.

After two weeks of dry, warm, sunny weather, the remaining dry grass was ready to explode into flames. For those of you have who have no experience with grass fires, let me tell you a very short story to provide perspective.

When I was seven, Buddy M (a neighbor boy) and I were playing in a big culvert by Murphy Stage Road, a heavily traveled highway near our houses. On a very hot, late-summer afternoon we saw a car go by and saw the passenger toss a cigarette out the window into the ditch which happened to be filled with, what else, 18-inch high dry grass. Nothing happened for about 30 seconds, so we went back to playing in the culvert.

Buddy and I soon heard what sounded like an explosion. We looked up to see a long stretch of the ditch ablaze with flames shooting 15 feet up into the air. The fire then jumped the road and was burning with flames 20 to 30 feet high closing at the top making a 100 yard stretch of the road look literally like a tunnel of fire.

When a big gas truck tried to run the fire gauntlet, Buddy yelled, "Hit the dirt!" We hugged the ground fully expecting a huge explosion as the speeding truck flew through the flames. But, all of that is really another story for another time. I just wanted the uninitiated to know what happens to dry grass when it reaches its kindling point—it explodes into flames.

Now Colby and I didn't expect to encounter near summer conditions in that field in late February. So Colby grabbed the burning red-rubber inner tube and scampered off through the field with me in hot pursuit, armed with only an oak branch I had picked up. With each fire I put out, two more started. When I got to them, the flames were about knee high, but by then there were four fires with flames waist high. Then, "Lord please help me," there was a wall of flames about 10-feet high moving toward me while Colby was on the other side of the flames having a great time setting more fires without even turning his head to appreciate the inferno he had created.

I wasn't worried at all about the new fires Colby was setting, because the wind was blowing toward me. So, any new fires would only burn back toward me until they hit the wet green grass (which was what was left in the wake of the big fire). Then, any new fire would die for lack of fuel. What I was worried about was how I was going to beat to death a raging grass fire with only an oak branch and no help from Colby. Heck, every time I hit the fire with the branch, it burned a little more of my fire-fighting equipment. My oak branch was starting to grow shorter very rapidly.

I yelled, "Colby, drop that infernal tube! We've got to get this fire put out now!"

That got his attention. As Colby turned he saw what I had already recognized all too clearly. This was a disaster with a capital "D" and that rhymes with "T" and that stands for total loss—the house that is

You see, the wind was moving the fire slowly and steadily toward Colby's house. His house was the little cabin by the woods that Colby's Great Uncle John and Aunt Ethel (I mentioned them in another story) gave to Colby's parents. The house was made of finely aged pine logs and time-cured cedar siding, all well seasoned wood that would go up like a box of matches if the fire got to it.

Well Colby didn't listen to everything I said. He did run around one end of the fire to get on the downwind side to help me stop its progress toward the house. But Colby had just stomped out the flames on the red rubber tube and, since he had no other firefighting equipment, he brought the red inner tube and started beating on the fire. His firefighting equipment started to shrink more rapidly than my oak branch and it started a few more fires before Colby threw the thing away.

By this time the fire was generating enough heat to do what many wild fires do, that is to create their own little meteorological regime, complete with a strong pressure gradient to really whip up the wind around the fire. The intensified wind made the fire hotter and it burned faster.

The heat got so intense that every time we stepped toward the fire to take a whack at it, we got burned a little. We had to step in, whack, and then retreat. So for the next few minutes it was step, whack, retreat, and repeat.

We were inhaling smoke, getting singed, and making no headway in slowing the fire's inexorable movement toward the house. Colby and I had long since used up our original fire fighting equipment and were picking up any stick, no matter how short, that we came across. Sometimes we even threw rocks at that fire. When we couldn't come up with anything to whack the fire with, we stomped it with our shoes. That maneuver usually earned us a burn or two.

At about this time I began to think it was a hopeless situation and I yelled, "It's no use, Colby! We can't stop it!"

As we both were about ready to throw in the towel due to exhaustion, frustration, and realization, we turned and looked helplessly, hopelessly at the little house. The sight of what used to be Uncle John's and Aunt Ethel's old house just sitting there at the edge of the field fueled a fierce determination in us. We had to stop that fire. It couldn't be allowed to burn up Uncle John and Aunt Ethel's house. They were two of the finest people we had ever known and no fire was going to take their house as long as there was life in either Colby or me.

We finally came across some slightly better sticks as we retreated toward the house and began a furious offensive against the fire. "Darn flames and straight ahead" was our battle cry. Flames licked at us and we kicked at them. We beat them. We even taunted them. We were fearless, and somehow, probably due to God's mercy, we beat that fire into submission with only about 10 feet of field left. It was a fight to the finish. It was nearly a photo finish, but we had won!

Even though Colby and I were beyond mere exhaustion, and even though we were about to puke from smoke inhalation, and even though our adrenaline flow was pushing us beyond our normal physical limits, we had the same thought at the same time and said simultaneously, "We can't let our parents know anything about this."

We looked for what ever we needed to do to cover our tracks, but the fire had burned so cleanly across the field that the few ashes created sank into the green wet grass near the ground and became invisible. So, after knocking down the few blackened stocks of dry grass that remained upright, we stumbled into the house and breathing heavily collapsed into a couple of big chairs. That was when we heard our folks pull in the driveway.

We both tried to look a little more relaxed before our parents came in the back door.

But, too tired to raise his head, Colby said between two heavy breaths, "Nothing like being just in the nick of time, huh?"

"A minute sooner and we would have been toast. Now they'll never know," I added, thinking how near we had come to becoming literal toast.

As our parents stepped into the room, we both raised our heads for the first time since entering the house ourselves and looked up at our Moms and Dads. The four of them stood there still and quiet for a few seconds. Then Colby's Dad asked, "Just what have you two been up to?"

Colby replied, "Dad, why do you think we've been up to something?"

To that Colby's Mom responded, "Both of you, go look in the mirror."

"What for?" Colby asked.

Though this was starting to look bad for us he was still not willing to concede anything.

"Just go look in the mirror," his Mom said again. This time it sounded more like in order than a suggestion.

A bit puzzled, we both pulled our fatigued bodies out of the chairs and drug ourselves over to the biggest mirror in the house, where we did a double take as our eyes focused on our reflections. Our hair was singed to the point that it looked like we had gray, frizzy Afro hair cuts. Colby's eyelashes were gray, mine were missing. Our eyebrows, or what was left of them, were also gray and frizzy. Something else we hadn't noticed was that we both stank like burned hair. We guessed that our parents had smelled that too.

Now we knew how our parents knew that something had happened. But we never really filled them in on all the details, thereby avoiding such harsh consequences as never being able to have a bonfire again—or, perhaps a trip to the woodshed.

As our adrenaline flow subsided, the burns we had sustained began throbbing, so we snuck into Colby's room to doctor them in secret. In his room we couldn't resist stepping in front of his mirror to see once again what we looked like after the fire had turned Colby and me into two grizzled old men.

15
The Bioterrorist

Why do some things that start so innocently end up being so vile? I never would've imagined that sharing a lesson in physics would've ended up creating the bioterrorist.

While growing up Colby and I, like all school kids, were taught at least some science every year. But it was usually watered down, boring, or was an afterthought buried in stuff that you read for your reading class.

The first really good science class I had was in the ninth grade. My science teacher, Mr. Ford, tried really hard to make his class interesting and even funny. He would let us do things in our labs that most teachers would cringe at, or just call the principal if they caught you. One of the more memorable periods in the lab was right after we had finished a lecture on electrostatic energy explaining how it can be used to create an electric current.

One piece of lab equipment that Mr. Ford let us play with was the electrostatic generator. It was a wheel turned by a hand crank. The device had brushes to generate static electricity and two metal balls on movable arms called electrodes that you could cause a small lightning bolt to jump between if you cranked hard enough and if you got the electrodes close enough together.

Well some of us guys discovered that if one guy grabbed the electrodes, one with each hand, and another guy turned the crank, electricity flowed right through the kid's body that was holding the electrodes. This discovery quickly degenerated into a contest to see which guy could stand the most electricity flowing through their body. There were three contestants. The first kid, Mike B, held on for about 20 seconds while we revved up the wheel pretty good with the crank. He let go with a loud yell. Then Gil M grabbed those two electrodes and we revved up that wheel for about 30 seconds. As soon as his body started shaking he let go. Finally Frank M grabbed the electrodes and we really cranked hard. I never realized how crazy Frank was until that moment. No matter how hard or long we cranked, Frank wouldn't let go. His hair was sticking out and his body was shaking and quivering all over, but he wouldn't let go. Then a horrifying thought came across our minds simultaneously—maybe Frank couldn't let go and we were killing him.

Well we stopped the wheel as fast as we could and when Frank was able to speak again his first words were, "Why did you guys stop? I was going for the record!"

You can see Mr. Ford wanted us to have fun in science class, although to be safe we did hold the electricity contest after he stepped out of the room for a few minutes. Even Mr. Ford had his limits.

Another thing that impacted me even more than I realized that the time, was a discussion of atmospheric pressure. You see I didn't know it, but I was destined to become a meteorologist (a research scientist in atmospheric physics) and this lesson was just whetting my appetite for what I would later become totally immersed in.

Mr. Ford's lesson told us about how barometers measure air pressure. Believe it or not, the 14.7 pounds per square inch that the atmosphere pushes in on us can drive a column of water up thirty-four feet. That's why mercury barometers proved to be more practical—the mercury gets pushed up only about 30 inches so you can read the barometer without having a fire truck with one of those extendible ladders on it.

I was showing Colby about how air pressure can easily hold up a column of water the height of a quart-sized Mason jar. I filled the jar with water by submerging it in a pool of water, being careful not to let the mouth of the jar get above water level, I lifted the water-filled jar upside-down pulling it out of the water up to, but not including the mouth, and it stayed filled with water. The water did not run out and no air got in.

I did not realize it at the time, but Colby's quick mind was already making many applications of the physical law I had just demonstrated—applications that went far beyond what I would have hoped for to things which I would come to fear.

To give you a hint of what Colby was thinking, he had been reading about early attempts by our nation and other countries at biological warfare. The agents being developed by various military research organizations were thought to be mostly designed to kill the enemy. Colby's response was, "Why not just incapacitate'm?" Then he added, "And it won't take millions of dollars of research either."

I have to claim complete ignorance of Colby's thinking and complete innocence of any participation in the development of the biological weapon because something unusual happened at that time. I can't remember just why, but I didn't see Colby for two whole weeks. After two weeks, we both thought it was about time to spend some time together, so I stayed over Saturday night at Colby's house.

It was a little before bedtime that evening when Colby said, "I've got something to show you—been working on it for two weeks."

He took me into his room. I was really curious until Colby pulled out a half-gallon sealed Mason jar—the kind you can pickles in. It looked like it was about one-quarter filled with water.

"What's so new about that?" I stated rather than asked. "I know, and you know, that we'll find a reason to build a bonfire tomorrow, then we'll throw that sucker in, like we always do, and in about twenty minutes it will blow glass shrapnel all over the county just like it always does."

"Hold on a minute," Colby interrupted. This stuff isn't going anywhere near fire or it will really explode and it won't take twenty minutes either."

That worried me so I cut to the chase, "Okay, what is it and what are we going to do with it?"

"Thought you'd never ask," Colby remarked with a self-satisfied, smirky tone to his voice.

"Remember that trick you showed me with a Mason jar full of water sticking up above the water level?"

"Yeah, the atmospheric pressure demonstration," I said gently correcting Colby.

"Yeah, whatever. The main point is that if you want to catch a gas in its concentrated form, with no air to dilute it, this is a way to do that."

"Yes you can do that if you've got a generator for that gas to generate the bubbles. Then, I suppose, you can catch the concentrated gas in the jar by guiding the bubbles into it," I said agreeing in principle with his point.

"So," I asked, "where's your generator?"

"It's me," was Colby's simple reply, a reply that unraveled the whole mystery to me.

I voiced the first thought that came to my mind, "Gross! How did you do that?"

"Well, I've been taking baths instead of showers for the last two weeks. Sometimes I take two baths a day. Of course I go outside and get dirty so Mom will tell me to go wash and then I wash up—I take a bath."

"But how did you get three-quarters of a big jar full of—" Colby cut me off at that point.

"I just keep complimenting Mom on her beans and she just keeps fixing them every night. Then, after dinner, I take a bath. You just have to be really careful not to let the mouth of the jar get above the water when you're catching bubbles," Colby explained, "or you'll ruin everything and have to start all over again."

I was amazed that he could be doing research to create a biological weapon right out in the open and no one even suspected. That must not be such a potent weapon after all I concluded.

"You mean to tell me that you have nearly a half gallon full of pure unadulterated gas?" I inquired with a bit of incredulity.

"Yep! An incapacitating biological weapon."

Now Colby could see that even though I might believe what was in the jar, I surely didn't believe it would incapacitate anyone. So without another word, Colby unscrewed the lid.

Since the flatus had long since been passed, the introduction of its highly concentrated product to the room was absolutely silent. The old phrase "silent but violent" couldn't even hold a candle to what happened next. We were in Colby's room, with the door and windows shut, while two weeks worth of his factory's production of weapons-grade gas diffused through the air at an incredible rate.

The result was foul. I felt contaminated. I could hardly breathe. I could see Colby having the same reaction as we both ran for the door.

Somehow I had the presence of mind to holler, "Don't hit the light switch or do anything that might make a spark or we're dead! And get the door shut behind us as quick as you can," I added as Colby exited the room right behind me scampering toward breathable air.

Well we made excuses to his parents as to why we didn't want to go to bed for a while. We also slipped outside and pried Colby's bedroom windows open from the outside. One more thing we did was spend quite a bit of the rest of the evening explaining to Colby's parents how fried chicken and mashed potatoes had such a deleterious effect on Colby and me and how that had made the whole house wreak like, well, you know what.

I don't know if Colby ever finished and mailed the letter we started drafting to the DOD that night. We emphasized to them our two primary conclusions. First, the biological agent was inexpensive. Second, it was sure to either incapacitate the enemy or send them running in retreat.

Since that night I have often wondered if in some remote place there are barracks of soldiers and a huge mess hall where the cooks make only pinto beans, and if there are bathtubs in every barracks with more sophisticated devices than Colby's big Mason jar. If so, it is all because of those two weeks when Colby became the bioterrorist.

The Canine Chronicles

There were two dogs in Colby's life while he was growing up. Colby and I loved them both but for different reasons—totally different reasons.

You may have seen the original, or the remake, of that movie, The Incredible Journey. You know that faithful dog that led the animals ever homeward? Well, that was old Nick—except you would have to add in the part about Nick's passionate hatred of snakes.

Pal, on the other hand, was just a fun-loving rascal—a rascal that could really run. You got an introduction to Pal, the pup, when you read "Pal Goes Forward."

How these two dogs impacted Colby's life and my life, is contained in their individual stories appropriately titled, "Old Nick," and "The Biscuit Eater."

16
Old Nick

Where he came from no one knew. Why he was here became common knowledge—like a guardian angel he was here to protect the people he was assigned to and he did that well. He was death on snakes. He was Old Nick.

He just wandered in one day from up in the mountains. Colby's Uncle John thought he might have been living as a wild dog, maybe with the coyotes. But, the truth is no one ever knew where he came from—just like Melchizedek in the Bible. Uncle John didn't choose that aspect of the dog's life when he named him or Colby and I would have had a mouthful to say when we called him, "Here Melchizedek, here Melchizedek!"

For some reason unknown to us, Uncle John named Nicodemus, after that Pharisee that was afraid of being associated with Jesus. Now Colby and I just didn't see that in Nicodemus—he wasn't afraid of anything. So we shortened his name to Nick. "Here Nick!" was easier on the tongue and it had a nice ring to it.

Now Old Nick saved people's lives many times. Heck, he saved Colby and me a time or two that we knew of. So, all those that knew him thought he might have been sent from heaven to act sorta' like a guardian angel. But snakes thought Old Nick came from the other place because he was "that other place" to them. Old Nick's hatred of snakes ran so deep that he killed every single snake he ever found, bar none, and Nick was very good at finding snakes. Whether it was a five-foot timber rattler or a nine-inch garter snake, Nick fought with and destroyed them all regardless of any danger to him.

When Colby and I headed into the woods, Nick faithfully took the point, protecting us from anything that might harm us. Many times Nick found rattlesnakes just before Colby and I walked past their hiding place under a bush or by a rock.

I will never forget the first time I saw Nick find a snake. Shortly after Uncle John and Aunt Ethel moved away and Colby's family moved into their house, Colby, A.J. and I were playing in the big field on the north side of the house (the one Colby and I later burned up—but that's another story you can read about elsewhere). I heard a low-toned combination of a growl and a bark. Immediately Colby yelled, "Snake! Run!"

Well I didn't know why I should run from a harmless snake. If it had been a rattler, it would have been buzzing loudly by now, so I didn't see any reason to run. About then a ferocious growl came out of Old Nick, almost like he had been transformed into some monster.

As I looked toward Nick I saw his head shake violently back and forth and I was showered by snake guts. It was downright revolting. You never know what gross stage of swallowing and digestion the snake's prey will be in when Nick slings it all over you. Colby and A.J., who had run a safe distance away, were laughing their heads off as they looked at those splotches of snake innards all over my clothes, face and arms—I called it getting "snicked." Colby knew what a gross out it was to get snicked because he had learned about Nick's snake neurosis the same way I had.

When Nick shook a snake they just cracked like a bull whip, only a snake's body ain't made of whip leather. Snake bodies are a lot softer, so when they crack like a whip, snakes pop apart. The sequence was Nick went snap, the snake went crack, then pop. All in all it was a quick and efficient, but very messy, execution.

In the summer, rattlesnakes were always a concern if you roamed the woods in southern Oregon. But, with Nick along, Colby and I never worried a bit about rattlesnakes (their guts maybe, but not the snakes themselves). I have come close to being bitten by rattlesnakes twice that I know of, but both of those incidents occurred after Old Nick had passed on to his eternal reward—a reward that Colby and I were positive he had earned and pretty sure that it existed.

We reasoned that there were probably connections between God and his creatures that people were unaware of—you know like God and Balaam's donkey. If God used any animal for good, we were sure that Old Nick was included with all such blessed creatures. After all, hadn't he saved Aunt Ethel's life when the frail, tiny lady was attacked by a big ram? The ram knocked her down and was moving in for the kill when Nick arrived and turned that goat every way but loose. He also saved her from a rattlesnake, just as he had Colby and me. Yes, Old Nick was bound for animal glory, whatever it was and wherever it was. Colby and I were sure of that.

One of our most memorable experiences with Old Nick started early one Sunday morning in spring when Colby and I thought we'd pick both of our Moms a bouquet of wild flowers. April and May brought blooming bird bills, tiger lilies, lamb's tongues, cat ears, Indian paint brushes, buttercups, bachelor buttons and, if you were lucky, you might find fragrant Easter seal lilies or azaleas.

Colby and I weren't particular, we were just gonna pick whatever we found first. But had we known what we would find first, well, it would have been the last thing we would have picked to find.

As we topped the first hill behind Colby's house and were about to cross the old power line road, now just a trail, we heard Old Nick growl and bark. That was followed by the loudest rattlesnake buzz we had ever heard.

We ran cautiously toward the ruckus because we weren't sure what we might run into and we sure didn't want to run between Nick and whatever rattler he had chosen to snap, crack and pop to reptile purgatory. Colby and I were sure that's where all dead snakes ended up even though our dads told us it wasn't scriptural. We thought it was because God is just—that is scriptural. So that's the way it had to be—purgatory—at least for rattlers and bull snakes.

As Colby and I rounded a bushy madrone that was trying to make a comeback from being whacked off by the power line road-building crew, what we saw made our blood run cold. Nick was death on snakes, but though he was all heart, he was just a mid-sized dog. The timber rattler, however, was by far the biggest of its species we had laid eyes on. He looked like he would be death on dogs.

Despite Nick's skill and experience, this fight just didn't look fair. The snake was between five and six feet long and its middle was as big around as my calf. When it coiled in the less-effective U shape it could still strike eight to ten feet and while striking it moved faster than my eyes could follow.

Colby had a lot of faith in Nick, but the monster snake's reach when it struck looked like it was just too far for Nick to defend himself. Nick couldn't get close enough for the kill without having to move seven or eight feet completely within the snake's striking range. This gave the venomous viper far too much time to hit Nick before the dog could retreat beyond reach.

The danger dawning on him, Colby yelled, "Here, Nick! Come here boy!"

He might as well have been yelling at the boulder that sat beside the old road for all the response he got from Nick. I didn't even see Nick flinch, turn his head, or anything to acknowledge that he'd heard Colby. Nick couldn't afford to—he kept all his attention focused on that snake where it needed to be if Nick was to have a chance of surviving this battle of deadly opponents—a battle that clearly demonstrated the degree of hate they had for each other. That rattler struck at Nick like a snake trying to get revenge for Nick's decimation of all the rattler's genus cousins.

Convinced that we could not dissuade Nick and mesmerized by the battle, Colby and I grew silent as the battle between super specimens of the two species wore on. Nick would bark, then charge in and the snake would strike from whatever striking pose it could get into. Nick would back out with lightning speed as the striking snake's fangs missed Nick's face by an inch or less. The movements of both animals were now so quick that they looked blurry even to our youthful eyes.

Tension built in Colby and me as we began to see what Nick would have to do. In order to win, and to be sure Nick would win (if winning was defined as killing the snake), Nick would have to expose his face, neck, and front legs to the rattler's venomous fangs in order to get an opportunity to clamp his jaws around the snake's thick neck. Even then, how could Nick shake to pieces something so thick and muscular that it weighed probably thirty pounds?

There was a story Colby and I had been told many times that came to my mind, "A healthy adult person seldom dies from a single rattlesnake bite. But, if they receive multiple bites, or a bite in a vulnerable spot, like the neck, they will probably die if they don't get help immediately." We were sure Nick would receive one or both of those fatal infusions from the fangs of the big timber rattler if he went in for the kill.

Well, Nick started another thrust at the snake, but this time the rattler was in the full-coiled position. As Nick back pedaled to about ten feet away, the powerful strike that followed caught him just above the eye. The faintest yelp came from Nick's mouth. That was followed by a fierce barking growl that was vintage Nick. Then Nick lunged for the snake's neck. The rattler had recoiled into the U position and struck Nick dead center on the front of the throat. But Nick just continued charging in and as the fangs loosened from his neck, Nick sunk his own fangs gum-deep into the rattler's neck, just below its head.

Now having the death grip he had sought all along, Old Nick began to shake that snake. Since he was holding a thirty pound snake, Nick's shakes were large in amplitude but very slow in motion at first. Slowly the frequency of the shakes increased and the big rattler, still buzzing, began to crack like a whip each time he changed direction. Crack, pop! There went the hindmost two feet of the snake. That stopped the rattling. Then Nick really began shaking that viper. Chunks of that snake flew all over Josephine County it seemed and snake guts splattered all over the place. Colby and I continued to keep our distance.

With the snake scattered all around him, Nick turned and ran to Colby with a happy whine and a tail that was wagging almost as hard as Nick had shaken the snake. Old Nick had won a monumental battle and he knew it. But at what cost?

Colby and I began to examine Nick for damage. There was a large open wound above his left eye and there were two big punctures in his neck. Both wounds concerned us so greatly that we headed back to Colby's house without as much as one flower between us. Our Moms would have no bouquets today.

Colby yelled for his Dad to come out as we approached the house. We tried to describe the battle to him and also Nick's two bites. He then checked Nick over and said, "There's not much we can do except watch him and wait."

These were not encouraging words to Colby. As we walked toward the little church next door to Colby's house for the morning service, both Colby and I noticed that the spring was gone from Nick's step. He found a cool shady spot and lay down, very still.

After the service Colby ran for the back door of the church house and sprinted toward his house.

"Here Nick! Here Nick!" he called, but there was no response.

I saw the concern growing on Colby's face and in his eyes. Both of us were worried nearly to death.

Colby was on the verge of tears when Old Nick drug himself out of the crawlspace under Colby's house and walked slowly toward us two boys. We were horror stricken at the sight we saw. Nick's throat had swollen so much that he looked like a bullfrog about to croak. I thought for sure Old Nick was going to croak too.

An involuntary yell came from Colby's mouth, "Dad!"

Colby's Dad quickly ended the conversation he was having with some of the church members and walked over to take a look at Nick. He saw Nick's throat and started to explain something to Colby.

As Nick was walking back toward the entry to the crawlspace, Colby's Dad said, "Son, Nick has had so many fights with rattlers over the years that he has probably been bitten several times before. So he's built up some immunity to the venom. We just have to leave him alone for a couple of days and he'll probably be fine."

Nick was just disappearing through the hole into the crawlspace when Colby began to sob. Crying is something that Colby and I just didn't do anymore, at least not so anyone would ever know. I figure Colby was thinking what I was thinking—all that swelling in Nick's neck was bound to be pressing hard on his wind pipe; how could he continue to breath if the swelling got worse?

The rest of the day was a somber time. Colby and I just sat around and worried. Our conversations were cursory, our reflections were restive. Nick was never mentioned that afternoon but he was never out of our thoughts.

My family had to leave for home at the end of the afternoon and Nick was still under the house. Colby's Dad was still consoling Colby with, "Leave him alone, Son, he'll be OK in a couple of days."

After what I'd seen I wasn't sure I believed that.

On Tuesday Colby's Mom called my Mom to talk like they often did. But I was handed the phone part way through the conversation. Colby was on the line.

"Hey, Col. How's things going?"

"Nick came out today."

"He did? How does he look?"

"Swelling's all gone. He has a big scab over his eye but he's OK!"

We both ended our part of the phone call smiling both inside and out. I guess Colby's Dad was right—he knew Nick just needed to rest while his rattler-reinforced immune system fought the poison that it had fought and defeated many times before.

That incident changed a lot of things. For one, Colby was finally convinced of Nick's mortality now and knew that someday he would lose his old protector and friend. That was probably why Colby asked for a puppy. He wanted a bloodhound—I think because of the fun we'd had chasing baying hounds that were chasing raccoons at the Powell's farm when we went hunting with them.

But about that bloodhound puppy, that's another story for a bit later.

With Nick back to full strength, we had many more adventures and Nick killed other rattlesnakes. He was never bitten again that we know of.

One morning a couple of years later, Colby went out to feed Nick and Colby's young hound. Nick was nowhere to be seen. He didn't come to the house at all that day.

In the early evening, Colby found Nick up on the hill behind their house. At the end, he had gone back toward the mountains from where he had first wandered in to Uncle John's place more than 16 years before. On that hillside was where Nick's body was laid to rest.

Colby cried a lot that day. I just felt a deep sense of loss that, as an old geezer, I sometimes feel even now. If the lion is gonna lay down with the lamb, heaven's got to have some animals. So I haven't given up hope of seeing Old Nick again some day. I sure hope that's the way God handles things for the good animals like Old Nick.

17
The Biscuit Eater

Pal and Old Nick were as different as night and day—well that's probably not the best metaphor to use. Instead, let's call them polar opposites. When you looked at Nick, you knew you were seeing wisdom incarnate. He knew what was right and Nick did it, no matter what the cost to him. To Pal, right wasn't a relative thing, it was just an irrelevant thing. He was, how shall I say this—emotionally incontinent. What I mean is that when Pal thought of something he wanted to do, most of the time he did it first, then, if it wasn't a good thing, he tucked his tail between his legs in dog shame later. The rest of the time he didn't even bother to tuck his tail between his legs—he just did what he wanted like a shameless biscuit eater.

When Nick had a close call from two rattlesnake bites, Colby finally realized that Old Nick was mortal. He decided to get another dog so he wouldn't be dog-less (something no country boy should be) when that dreaded day came for Nick to leave us. Colby went for a bloodhound puppy. I'm not sure that he appreciated the effort it takes to make a good hunting dog out of the impulsive, hormonal puppies that comprise the population of young hounds. But Pal was fun because he was so looney.

I think Colby and I had a lot more fun with Pal than we had training sessions.

Now, Nick was in his wise, golden years at this time, so he did help us train Pal a bit. Whenever Pal tried his silly puppy antics on Old Nick, Nick was not patient. If Pal's behavior was wrong, or annoying, Nick just growled and nipped the impetuous pup as frequently as needed to teach Pal the lesson Pal needed to learn. For the most part, Pal was a slow learner. But, stealing food from Nick's bowl—well, Pal learned right quick that he shouldn't do that.

As Pal began his first growth spurt, Colby and I could tell he was going to have long legs—way longer than most hounds. Those long legs were going to give Pal tremendous speed. That speed would turn out to be both a boon and a bane.

As for the biscuit eating indictment I made against Pal, he was guilty on two counts. The first count was from all the biscuits Pal ate—he was a literal biscuit eater. He loved biscuits more than his dog food or any other table scraps I can think of.

Colby and I made good use of Pal's biscuit-eating weakness for entertainment purposes. When there were several biscuits left over from a meal, before feeding them to Pal and Nick, we would dig some big night crawlers. Then we'd poke them inside some biscuits and offer them to Nick and Pal.

Nick was a temperate dog. He would sniff the biscuit. If it was laced with worm, he passed on it. Pal, on the other hand, gobbled up worm-filled biscuits as fast as we could give them to him. Colby and I roared in laughter as we got Pal to eat night crawlers and sometimes even grosser creatures. Over the years I would say we fed Pal more worms than we did the trout in southern Oregon. That was Pal the literal biscuit eater.

Pal was, on the second count, a figurative biscuit eater. Ever since Stuart Heisler directed that 1940 movie, <u>The Biscuit Eater</u>, the phrase has been with us in America. When a blood hound wasn't good for hunting because they only hunted for food, the hound was called a "biscuit eater." Sometimes such hounds would only hunt for food from the kitchen, food like left over biscuits—that was Pal. On that count, Pal was not only indicted, but he was tried and, on the testimony of many witnesses, convicted and sentenced to a hunting-less life.

Colby and I learned very quickly not to take Pal into the woods with us when we went hunting. Pal was always sniffing the ground and barking about something—usually nothing that we wanted to hunt. Well all that barking set off all of the human detection alarms in the woods. The digger squirrels—how we hated those little rat-like varmints—would start their piercing, shrill cry of "eeeeenchut, eeeeenchut!" This alert carried for a mile or more in the woods even to the human ear. Then there were those blasted blue jays. They would start their raspy, "aaaaank, aaaaank! This was an alarm that said to all forest inhabitants, "Quick, hide! Two boys with rifles and one biscuit-eating hound are coming!"

We quickly learned to leave Pal at home when we went hunting. But one place we could take Pal was the swimming hole—not when we were gonna fish too, but just when we were gonna go swimming.

It was on one of these swimming trips that we learned how fast Pal really was. On a hot Sunday afternoon, Colby's folks, my parents, and all of the kids piled into Colby's Dad's pickup and headed for Roger's hole (our swimming hole in Sucker Creek, the cold fork of the Illinois River). As we rolled down Cemetery Road (they call it Laurel Drive these days) with all of us kids in the back of the truck, we noticed Pal right behind us. At twenty-five miles per hour, Pal was easily loping along with us. The road got worse as we turned onto the old road that took us to the river and Pal slowed to a trot to keep pace.

When we reached the river, Pal joined us for a swim. This is where we learned something else about Pal; he was a master "shaker soaker." Not only could he really let the water fly when he wanted to dry off, but he had a knack for sneaking up on the least aware person and soaking them with drops of wet-dog scented water.

As we drove home from Roger's hole, Pal followed behind, but when we reached the pavement of Cemetery Road, Colby asked his Dad to speed up—he sped up to 35 miles per hour and Pal easily ran with us just behind the rear bumper. So we asked Colby's Dad to speed up to 45 miles per hour. Pal, with his long legs, kept pace without running all out.

Colby then piped up, "Dad, let's see how fast he can go!"

As the pickup slowly increased its speed to 50 miles per hour, Pal began running all out. At 50, we ran out of road and had to slow down to turn in to Colby's driveway. But, Pal kept up with us at each speed increment up to our max of 50 miles per hour. Pal could run like the wind!

Now I don't know if you've ever seen a greyhound run up close. I have—it's a thing of beauty. I was working on my throwing arm at the park once when some folks with two greyhounds came to give their dogs a workout. One person held the dogs, the other walked about 200 yards away across the flat, grassy park. On a signal, the first dog started his run. I was about midway between the two owners when the first dog passed by a mere fifteen feet from me. It ran like a line had been threaded through the dog's nose, down its spine and out its tail—like the line was stretched taut between the two people. There was no bobbing or wobbling, only the feet and legs of the greyhound moved. I could feel the force of its feet on the ground as they pounded by me—the ground shook enough for me to feel it. A greyhound running at nearly fifty miles per hour is indeed a thing of beauty. With only the feet and legs moving, the nose, body and tail fly like an arrow to its mark.

When Pal ran, he sorta' had the same motions as a greyhound. The way Pal moved his legs while running was the same efficient movement as a greyhound. But that's where the similarities ended. Pal's body rocked back and forth if you viewed him from the side. But the biggest difference was that Pal had a happy puppy face as he ran—his tongue flapped out of one side of his mouth and slobbers flew from it. Greyhounds ran all business like, but Pal ran for sheer youthful joy. He loved to run and he didn't give a rip what he looked like when he was doing it.

Running lit up Pal's eyes like nothing else but maybe a worm-filled biscuit. But, running also shut Pal's eyes.

One day Colby and I were playing in a creek near Cemetery Road when Colby's Dad came up the road in his old Ford, returning home from work. Pal saw that familiar car and ran to meet it. Fearful he wouldn't catch it, Pal gave a tremendous leap over the roadside ditch and lurched forward onto the road. This flung him in front of the front bumper of the car. Since Pal was only visible to Colby's Dad at the last second, he couldn't slow much and had no time to dodge Pal. So Pal took a bumper really hard to the head.

Colby's Dad stopped as quickly as he could, but Colby was already running toward his dog that lay stretched out and motionless on the road. Pal's speed had been his undoing. We carefully loaded Pal's body into the trunk of the car and drove the short distance to Colby's house. I could see Colby already resigning himself to digging a second grave up on the hill by Old Nick.

With Colby sobbing now, and me quiet, we pulled into the Ford's parking spot and prepared to prepare Pal for his funeral and burial. Colby's Dad opened the trunk so we could lift Pal out and Pal came flying out into Colby's arms, licking him on the face. We found out something else about Pal that day—he has a really hard head—literally!

Pal ran with Colby and me through the woods, to the swimming hole, and many other places, never protecting us as Nick had done, but having a lot of fun anyway.

After Colby moved to the little white house, one of the neighbor boys, Ronnie K, had a small motorcycle with a two-cycle engine. That bike had a droning, raspy, grating, buzzing sound that evidently grated on Pal's nerves. He tried to chase the bike away at every opportunity.

One day, as Ronnie K left Colby's house on his motorcycle, Pal heard that nerve-grating noise and took out after him from a side angle, sorta' like a defensive back closing in from the side on a running back who had gotten open and was headed for the goal line. Pal was fast and so Ronnie K didn't score a touchdown—he scored a broken leg instead. Once again Pal's eyes were closed from the accident. This time more than Pal's hard head was involved, and so Pal's eyes remained closed permanently. Pal earned himself a grave on another hill behind another house some six miles from Old Nick's grave on the opposite side of the river valley. That was appropriate for two dogs so opposite from each other in life. Colby had not lost a self-sacrificing, faithful friend like he had in Nick, but he had lost a friend that lived for the sheer joy of living. He had lost the hound that never learned to hunt, but a friend that had eaten so many worm-filled biscuits that I called him, the biscuit eater.

18
Rocks Can Rock'n Roll

Now, when Colby and I were growing up, most of what was called rock and roll music wasn't. Not at all! Even "I Dig Rock and Roll Music," by Peter, Paul and Mary was just a folk song. Most of the late fifties and early sixties music wasn't really that rebellious genre of music called rock and roll. It was mostly just harmless bubble gum music. It wasn't particularly edifying, but it was relatively harmless. But it wasn't so harmless when we discovered that rocks can rock'n roll.

This story has its roots in something Colby and I discovered that we could do to liven up our treks to the limestone caves. You see, about half way to the caves the old road runs along the top of a huge mountainside meadow. The meadow extends at least three hundred yards down the mountainside and has a very steep descent.

This meadow was in an area where there are a lot of rocks. The road was almost solid rock at this point. It was cut right into the side of the mountain through a bunch of serpentine which glistened in the afternoon sun flaunting its dazzling green hues.

The meadow itself was punctuated with rocks of all sizes, just laying there on the surface of the ground—waiting.

Now to Colby and me, all those punctuation marks looked like periods and they begged for words to preface them. We thought we could hear the rocks cry out with imperative sentences (which end with periods) saying stuff like, "Push me. Roll me. Help me smash something."

Since these words came as commands, who were we to disobey the talking rocks? Besides, the Bible says that if the people won't do what God says, then the rocks will cry out. Well they were crying out, so maybe Colby and I were supposed to do something—something like pushing them.

One day I stepped off the road onto the hillside meadow below, selected a round rock about the size of a basketball, and obeyed the "Push me" command.

Colby and I both watched the rock accelerate from the gravitational force. Though it began with a slow roll, the rock soon started bounding, chewing up thirty feet or more at a jump and chewing up the dirt wherever it hit. Traveling at fifty miles per hour or more, the rock hit the vegetation below and chewed a lot of it up as wild crashing noises tickled our boyish ears which then begged to be scratched with more such noises.

Colby and I spent a couple of hours looking for bigger and still bigger rocks to roll down the mountain. We loved the feeling of unleashing such raw power and we loved hearing the rocks convert their kinetic energy into so many different types of delightful crunching sounds. Yes we loved it but, if plants have emotions, the vegetation below hated it.

Well that's how Colby and I started rolling rocks. The rockin' part came later when I taught my rock rolling skills to some of my friends.

The year I graduated from high school, the twins, Don and Vaughn B, as well as Jerry D and Wayne W all had motorcycles. We decided that we would try to go down the Rogue River to the wilderness area during our spring break. We planned to ride the dirt road that followed the ridge line on the north side of the river. Some other friends of ours, Dale W and Jon W (along with a few of their friends) were going to hike the famous Rogue River Trail down into the wilderness area. Our coordinated plan was to rendezvous wherever the road, the trail, and the terrain made it possible to do that.

For the uninitiated, the Rogue River Trail starts near a place called Galice, at the mouth of Hell's Gate Canyon. The trail follows one of the wildest and most scenic white water rivers in the world through the coastal mountains on the river's course to the sea. This area has been made famous by writers, such as Zane Grey, and by several Hollywood movies, such as the John Wayne film, <u>Rooster Cogburn</u>.

When Colby and I were still tweens, some crazy loggers with money and wet winters to burn started building white-water hydroplanes and challenging each other to races on the Rogue and Klamath rivers. White water hydroplane racing was not a safe sport, but it evolved into something called the Boatnik. In this race, thirty or more propeller-driven hydros, with the biggest engine the boat owner could adapt for this use bolted on the back, and a hull especially designed for river racing would converge on Grants Pass Memorial Park on Memorial Day. They would race thirty miles down river and back to the park.

These guys were absolutely crazy. I saw one logger with a Corvette engine on the back of his boat going through Hell's Gate at speeds of up to one-hundred miles per hour. He could hardly steer between the rocks at that speed. Needless to say, the attrition rate in the Boatnik was high. Since boats of that time were propeller driven, most ended up adrift in the river after sheering off their props on rocks. Many times only three or four boats finished the race out of the thirty plus boats that started.

Well we aimed to ride our motorcycles past Hell's Gate and clear down to Agnes (about fifty miles down river) passing through the wilderness area as we went.

Don B and I decided we should ride until about 5 PM, stop somewhere for the night, and then try to rendezvous with the hikers sometime on the second day out.

We continually reminded each other to be on the lookout for hermits. Many old codgers in the area preferred the solitary life. So, they filed claims along the creeks that ran into the Rogue. Most of them panned enough gold to eke out a living. They were known for shooting people who wandered too near their claims. Wandering too near was something we wanted to be careful not to do.

All of us bike riders carried packs with sleeping bags, food, and water for the trip. It had been a cold winter and we encountered a few patches of snow along part of the ridge as we rode that afternoon. Shelter was foremost on our minds. About 4 PM, Don spotted a cabin sitting at an odd angle just below the road.

"No signs of life that I can see," Don B said confidently.

"It doesn't even look livable," I added. But "livable" wasn't a sufficient criterion to rule out inhabitation by some old hermit geezer.

The five of us parked our bikes on the road and crept down toward the cabin. As we got within fifty yards or so of it we could see that not only was it not inhabited, but it appeared to have slid off its foundation and then slid part way down the mountain until its progress was halted by some trees. Since it had a roof, and since this story takes place in mid March, the cabin would certainly beat sleeping out in the open.

We had made good time on our first day out, so we declared the cabin "home" for the night. We hid our bikes and got our camping gear. The cabin sloped downhill so steeply that it was hard to keep our heads up hill after falling asleep. We all woke up numerous times with our heads down hill and blood rushing to our brains. But, in spite of telling yarns and pulling pranks, we got some sleep during the course of the night.

Morning dawned bright with a partly cloudy sky. After breakfast all five of us went exploring down the hill toward the river (which was still well over 1,000 feet below us). We hadn't gone far when we came upon a huge meadow on the hillside. Guess what? It was punctuated with numerous rocks of all sizes and the rocks were once again speaking to me, "Push me! Please push me!"

A short pep talk on the fun and excitement of rolling rocks soon won all the guys over. I pushed the first rock, about basketball size. It accelerated, traversed the 300 yard meadow quickly, and began crashing in the trees and brush below. The crashing went on for what seemed like a full minute and then terminated with a big splash some 1,200 feet below us.

By that time all the guys were hooked. We all started pushing every rolling-rock candidate in sight. The din from breaking limbs, small landslides, and splashing into the river was nearly continuous until we started running out of rocks.

I started looking for a rock that could serve as our grand finale. There was one large outcropping in which a portion of it jutted up 8 feet or so—half again the size of a large refrigerator. It looked immovable. Nevertheless, I went over and examined it. The huge rock was cracked around the base, but still looked firmly connected to whatever part lay buried under the mountainside. I was about to walk away but decided to push on it a little just to be sure it really was immovable.

I gave it a good hard push and it appeared to move, but so slightly that I thought I was seeing what I wanted to see rather than reality. I pushed once more nearly as hard as I could. The rock did move, but the movement was barely perceptible.

"Hey guys! Come check this out," I called to Don, Vaughn, and the others.

When they arrived I suggested, "Don, why don't you and I push and the rest of you guys tell us what you see."

Don and I pushed on the rock and the rock moved. I had picked Don because, even though he looked like a scrawny 115 pounder, he had been a state champion wrestler two years before and I personally had seen him lift 1,600 pounds with his legs.

At this point excitement began to build. In our imaginations we could already see this juggernaut tearing a path all the way to the river. I sent Wayne W and Jerry D to get something we could use as a lever while the rest of us tried to break the rock free. After Wayne and Jerry returned with a large pole taken from the cabin, we brought all our strength and leverage to bear against this boulder. We moved it—it broke free!

All we had to do was push it over the square edge that was keeping it from rolling on its own and that gargantuan boulder would be free to do what all rocks really want to do—crush everything in their path until all their kinetic energy is spent.

We all bore down as hard as we could and the rock rocked.

"I think we need a little rockin' if we're gonna roll," I quipped.

So we started rocking that immense monolith. As we rocked it, we found that if we kept doing that repeatedly, the amplitude of the rocking increased. So we kept rockin' that rock until it rolled, and let me tell you, then things really rocked!

The boulder did a couple of slow rotations that made a deep "whump, whump" sound. Our feet could feel the ground shake with each whump. Next that sucker started picking up speed, then came the bounding part—I just love that part.

The rock was bouncing along at about 30 feet between points of impact with the earth. At each collision with the ground, dirt flew out all over the place. But to our horror, the rock was heading straight toward a 100-foot high pine tree at the far end of the meadow. We thought our fun was going to end before the crashing din down below and the big splash in the river could ever happen.

Well the boulder took a huge leap, knocked about half of the dirt off the side of the mountain and then leaped again. It was still about 10 feet in the air when it made a direct hit on that pine tree. The pine tree cracked like a whip with the wave traveling all the way up the tree trunk to the top. There, just like at the end of a huge bull whip, the top of the tree cracked. It cracked so hard that the topmost 15 feet broke off, flew out like a giant spear, and stuck into the ground.

Meanwhile the rock recoiled from its collision with the tree, bouncing back up the hill about 10 feet or so and then started a second run down the mountain.

We all began to cheer as the rock continued its trip down the mountain toward the Rogue River. The boulder disappeared quickly into the brush far below us but the crashing only intensified in volume as the rock once again felt the acceleration of gravity call it down to its final resting place.

Vaughn B started a cheer, "Splash, splash!" We all joined in. "Splash, splash, splash, splash!" We continued to cheer rhythmically until our ears were rewarded with a big "KERPLOOOOSH" which sounded deep and loud as it echoed up and down the river canyon for several seconds.

Instinctively, at the conclusion of the echoing splash, we all ran down to examine the damage created by the first part of the boulder's trip.

I ran to where we saw all that dirt explode off the side of the mountain. When I got there I was horrified, first by one thing, then by another.

The first horrific sight was caused by the realization that we were only 250 to 300 yards above the Rogue River Trail and we didn't even realize it. The trail was nicely cut out of the side of the mountain and well maintained by forestry crews. The explosion of dirt we saw was the boulder wiping about 20 feet of the trail right off the side of the mountain. The trail just stopped; there was a 10-foot cut out of the mountainside and then the trail resumed about 20 feet beyond that.

If we were caught I was sure we would be arrested, fined some obscene amount, and then I would be doing community service for the rest of my life—so much for my scholarship to the U of O. My life would be over.

The shock of those thoughts was causing me to not really recognize what my eyes were seeing just up the trail about 50 yards.

About then, Don yelled, "Let's get out of here!"

He probably yelled that not so much from fear of the punishment if we were caught as from the fact that just up the trail were five guys in the prone position with their rifles trained on us.

I was shocked, frozen in place, couldn't seem to move. But neither were the riflemen moving. I didn't know if that was a good sign or a bad one. Were they some sort of paramilitary group about to shoot us or take us captive? Or, were these young hermits about to shoot us as trespassers?

Just then one of the guys behind a rifle with a big scope waved to me. I distinctly heard him say to his cohorts, "It's OK, nobody's trying to kill us." Then I recognized our friends. They also had made good time and were miles further than we had anticipated down the trail—the trail we had knocked off the side of the mountain—the trail where we had just about crunched our friends with an avalanche of rocks.

Well we had a reunion with Dale W, Jon W, and the others. It was filled with thankfulness. We were thankful that, in our carelessness, we had not killed them and they were thankful that there wasn't an old hermit trying to get rid of them via an avalanche.

I vowed right there never to roll rocks where there was even a remote possibility of hurting people or property. We were never arrested for what we did to the trail. I figure the forest rangers, with their crew of young would-be rangers, probably fixed the trail as part of their regular spring trail maintenance.

Though I never rolled rocks like that again, I still gotta' say, "Man, rocks can rock'n roll and that really rocks!"

19
The City Slicker

He ran smack dab into trouble but he didn't recognize it even though it stared him right in the face. By that time, he had already irrevocably made what might prove to be the biggest mistake of his young life. What the mistake was, and how it all came to be, is what this story is all about. But, be it known to all that it was the kind of mistake that would only be made by the city slicker.

The story starts with some friends Colby and I made because of one of those unusual things our church believed. You see we believed that you should have communion every Sunday at our church and we did it just like you read it in Mark 14:22, where Jesus "…took the bread gave thanks and broke it." Now that's plain enough. You just pick up the bread, pray and then break it. It's a no brainer! But our friends' parents believed you shouldn't break the bread because the bread symbolizes Jesus' body and no bones in his body were ever broken. So as far as agreeing on this point, we were at an impasse. This meant that our two groups could never have church together on Sunday morning. But Sunday afternoon was fair game. Because the only bread to be broken then was not communion bread, rather it was cinnamon rolls, or maybe some biscuits. Therefore, many times families from the two churches would get together and have Sunday sings, visit, eat a lot of good food, and the kids would play until we dropped.

Now, on this particular afternoon, we had met with several families at the Powell's place for one of those Sunday sings. The Powell's owned a dairy farm off Holland Loop Road. The Mom, Dad and kids ran the dairy. The Grandfather had all the hay fields and barns to store the hay in to provide feed for the dairy cows. The area that the Powell's dairy and hay fields covered was huge. There were nine or ten hay fields as well as the dairy itself. Their land, owned plus leased, stretched clear across the river valley and it included many groves of trees, creeks and other great habitat for all sorts of wild animals.

Colby and I ran with the Powell kids through nearly all of that land as we played tag, hide and seek, and other games we made up. Sometimes the Powell men would take Colby, me and the older Powell kids with them coon hunting with their hounds. Running full speed through the fields and trees on a misty moonlit night in pursuit of baying hounds that, in turn, were hot on a raccoon's trail was enough to make Colby and me think we had died and gone to heaven. To us, the Powell's place was nearly heaven on earth—until the city slicker came.

The city slicker's name was Donald. Don't go thinking he was a bad kid, because he wasn't. He was just a cousin of the Powell's that had lived in L.A. for all of his 10 years. He was so ignorant that he had to see milking time at the Powell's dairy before he would believe that milk wasn't just made in a factory and put into cartons.

Donald was a few years younger than Colby and me. But within a few minutes, to his delight, he had been fully accepted into the group and was playing tag with the kids on the large front lawn. Our game of tag got modified several times until, in early evening, it took way more room to play than the Powell's front yard had. So we moved out into the nearest hayfield, which had been recently cut. It was like a giant lawn, 200 yards long and about 100 yards wide.

Just as we started to play Colby yelled, "There goes a skunk!"

That's all it took to send a passel of kids off to chase a skunk as far as we could run it. Colby and I had a lot of experience at skunk chasing. We knew when to pursue, when, and at what distance, to circle (if the skunk stopped), and when to break off the chase because the skunk showed signs of extreme irritation.

We thought all kids had developed enough survival skills to know that there are certain things you just don't do with a skunk. We surmised correctly for all the kids except the city slicker. Neither Colby nor I realized our error until was too late.

Shortly after sunset we chased the harried skunk across the third hayfield when the polecat made a beeline for an oak tree at the edge of a grove of trees.

Quickly perceiving the skunk's strategy I yelled, "Colby, the tree is hollow!"

Upon that Colby and I screeched to a stop. All the rest of the kids were running a short distance behind us and they stopped too—all but the city slicker.

Donald ran at full speed past our vantage point some 25 yards from the tree. Colby and I were so flabbergasted that we were dumb struck.

My brain was telling my mouth, "Warn the kid! Do it now!" But, being struck dumb, my paralyzed mouth just couldn't respond in the three or four seconds it took Donald to reach the tree and stick his head into that gas chamber.

I've got to pause briefly at this point to provide some technical information for the non-meteorologists who are reading this story. As the sun sets on a summer evening in a river valley, there's this phenomenon known as a temperature inversion that sets up very quickly. An inversion is sort of like a lid on top of the air that doesn't let pollen, smoke, bad smells, or in anything suspended in the air move upward. That nasty stuff can only move out to the sides. Right after sunset, this inversion can remain six feet or so off the ground for a while. This means that anything released into the air near the ground can remain very, very concentrated. For example, people with allergies go nuts if pollen or molds are being released. Bad odors can stink just as bad several hundred yards away as they did it right where they originated.

It was just after sunset when Donald chased the skunk into the hollow tree and took a skunk toot to his snoot. Now about skunk smells—when Loudon Wainwright III wrote that song a few years later called "Dead Skunk in the Middle of the Road"…"and it stinks to high heaven," he knew what he was talking about. A dead skunk can really stink. But when a skunk voluntarily sprays those dreadful droplets directly from its stink glands, the smell is many times stronger. Heck, under the right conditions, it can make a grown man 50 yards away puke his guts out. But, when the skunk is cornered, and is in a panic, it squirts more juice and the odor is simply incredible.

Now when Donald stuck his head into the hollow tree and saw the skunk's rear end, the panicked skunk gave Donald everything it had—right in Donald's face. I know this to be true, because from my angle, about 25 yards away, I could see the globules of spray making contact with Donald's eyes, nose, and mouth.

Well Donald was just a little boy, not a man, and he was less than 50 centimeters away, not 50 yards away, so he more than just puked his guts out.

First there was a loud scream as the high PH base that served to hold the skunk stench burned Donald's eyes and nose. Then came the involuntary vomiting. Wretched Donald retched his way all the way back to the farm house, using the moments between his vomiting to cry and scream simultaneously. It was the pitiful sound of a child in agony and it brought every Mom in the house running into the yard fearing their child was the one doing the wailing.

Meanwhile, growing nauseous from the odor, I began to sprint directly away from the place of the incident to a creek about one-quarter mile away. Not to be bragging, but I'm pretty fast. For many years I was the sprint champion of our city. But not even my speed was enough to outdistance the skunk smell. Molecular diffusion can transfer airborne molecules more quickly than one might think. I got to the creek, took a breath of what I hoped would be fresh air, but only got the fresh scent of skunk. My stomach was quivering and on the verge of hurling, so I plunged my head into the cool fresh creek water. At last no smell of skunk, but neither could I breath. So back into the gas chamber my head went. Well I bobbed repeatedly for a moment or two before deciding to run further away and then circle in a big arc back to the farm house.

Upon arriving at the farm house, Donald ran into the yard making a beeline straight for his Mom. But evidence of what had transpired reached his Mom before Donald did—via her olfactory organs.

As Donald's Mother held him at arms length—I might add a note here to all Moms—never give in to the temptation to hug your kids when they come crying because they have been sprayed by a skunk because the hug won't help your kid and, believe me, you'll really regret it if you do. The only thing that will help is to lower the pH of the entire kid about three points or so on the pH scale and for that you need a mild acid, like tomato juice.

Well as Donald's Mom held him at bay, Grandma Powell had already grabbed her old galvanized tub. Grandma then ran to the pantry and wrapped her arms around as many jars of canned tomatoes as she could hold. By then another lady had grabbed a hose and Donald's Mom had ripped every stitch of clothing off from her kid.

Modesty was not even a consideration here. So we all stood and watched nude Donald get shoved into the tub. I'm sure he'll cringe for the rest of his life each time he remembers that even his girl cousins saw him buck naked that day. Well his Mom had no more than shoved Donald into the tub when the first jar of tomatoes from Grandma Powell splattered over his head. Many more jars followed as did many blasts from the hose.

After the first panicked tomato washing, Donald was bathed more meticulously in tomato juice twice more before showering and getting dressed in clean clothes. Now, at least, there was no more puking.

Because Donald still smelled, the kids were all reluctant to play with him when he emerged all scrubbed up and in clean clothes. But pretty soon we all realized how easy on the nose that light lingering skunk smell was compared to what we had first smelled after the explosion from the skunk's scent glands and so Donald was again accepted into our games.

Yes, Donald started the afternoon as an ignorant kid from the city, but after the experience he gained that day, Colby and I had a new respect for Donald. He had earned acceptance, albeit the hard way, and therefore Colby and I would never again call him the city slicker.

20
Old Wet Dynamite

Colby sat behind me on the seat of my little Honda motorcycle as we headed down the mountain toward Cave's Highway on the bumpy dirt road. Behind us, the road ascended steeply up to a partially logged off forest of fir trees where we had discovered a deserted logging landing—and the old wet dynamite.

Excitement and skepticism were intermingled in our conversation.

"Why would they just throw it away," Colby questioned incredulously.

"Probably because it got wet," I surmised. "It looks like they were trying to hide it by tossing it all over that big log at the edge of the clearing."

"Maybe so, but I bet they're not coming back for it now. All of the sticks are wet and they're unraveling. It's been there quite a while. Nobody wants that stuff," Colby reasoned.

"You're right," I concluded.

"But maybe we do," Colby interjected, contradicting himself.

That was when we reached consensus—the moment where excitement trumped skepticism. Right then we firmly believed that saturated dynamite could somehow "keep its powder dry" and not behave like a dud firecracker. We were so ignorant!

Without saying a word, I made a slow u-turn at a wide spot in the road, down shifted and headed back up the mountain with the little Honda engine wound tight in low gear. It was a tough job for a little 50 cc engine to pull us both up the steep hill.

Our intent for sure was to get the dynamite. But I didn't know how we could possibly carry that crumbling mess to Colby's house without a scoop shovel and a wheelbarrow.

A few minutes later we parked my bike at the landing and ran over to look behind the log. There it laid, a mass of mush, oozing a bit and smoking lightly—nearly a case of deteriorating dynamite.

"Got anything we can stuff this in?" asked Colby.

"Let me check my saddlebags."

I nearly always kept two saddlebags slung over the gas tank on my little Honda Sport. So, I dug deep into one side and pulled out two brown paper bags.

"How about two big grocery bags? That's all I've got to put it in."

Colby thought for a moment and replied, "Better double the bags. We can fill them and just leave what ever won't fit."

Considering it was over 10 miles back to Colby's place, I knew we'd be lucky to get a large grocery bag full of wet dynamite back home intact. If we'd known the truth, it was only by God's grace that we made it back intact.

You see, old wet, sweating dynamite, oozing so much nitroglycerin that it appears to be smoking, is so volatile that dropping it or even jostling it too hard can set it all off. Do you know what an explosion of a grocery bag full of exuding dynamite mush can do? I didn't know then, but I learned—very soon—experientially.

Just to be "safe" we carefully scooped the mush into the double bags using a flat piece of wood. Nothing happened during the bag filling except the material smoked a little more and the bag grew very, very heavy. At the three quarters point we were afraid the double bag might rip and dump our load, so we stopped filling it.

I hopped onto the front of the Honda seat. Colby slipped to the very back part of the seat and put his arms around my waist, wedging the bag tightly between us. Off we rode down the bumpy road toward the highway. We were two ignorant boys headed most likely toward early graves, provided there would be anything left to put in a grave.

I would really have hated it if Colby and I had taken a spill, hit a big bump, or if the bags had ripped while going 50 miles per hour down the highway. Think about it! How would you like to try to explain your premature arrival at the Pearly Gates to St. Peter, and then try to convince him to let you in by pleading innocence or ignorance, or some other such nonsense?

I can just hear St. Peter, "You two boys are not innocent. You took something that didn't belong to you—something that could blow you two to kingdom come. As a matter of fact it did. By the way what were you and Colby planning to do with that stuff?"

The answer to that hypothetical question is the rest of the story—the part where we learned about old dynamite—experientially.

You see the dynamite wasn't the only abandoned thing we knew about. In the woods about three-quarters of a mile up a dirt road from Colby's house was a 1930 something Chevy. It was on blocks, mostly stripped, but the engine block was still in it and the hood was still on. Today that shell would be worth a fortune because of the body, frame, and engine block. In 2009, such a find would be a classic car buff's dream. But to Colby and me, it was just something that begged to be blown up. Our ambition was the complete demolition of the old car.

We had already tried saltpetre and sugar based explosives, but they just didn't have enough bang. Colby said that if the dynamite wasn't a dud, we could reduce that car to shrapnel with a few carefully placed charges. I hoped he was right, but the thought of shrapnel made me duck.

Mercifully, we made it back to Colby's place without incident. We didn't stop at the house, but just continued up the old road that skirted Colby's parent's land and angled toward Rockydale Road. We turned onto a smaller road that went deeper into the woods. We arrived at the abandoned car safely and hid our dynamite in a dry place nearby (as if that mattered, but we thought it did).

Nothing would get blown up today because it was late in the afternoon and we still needed some supplies for the demolition project.

"I think five or six blasting caps and about 25 feet of fuse will do it," Colby estimated out loud.

"Probably so, but just where do you plan to get them? At the five and dime?" I said sarcastically.

"I know a guy who's Dad's a logger. He gets things for himself and for his friends whenever he wants. His Dad's got such a stash of blasting supplies that he never seems to miss a little fuse or a few blasting caps. Dynamite sticks, he tracks a little more closely, but we don't need to worry about where the dynamite is going to come from," Colby explained.

I laid out my concerns very logically, "I've got two questions: number one, does he consider you a friend of his; number two, do you really believe the old wet mush will explode?"

"First," Colby answered, "Yeah, he's friend enough to get the stuff, especially if he gets to watch what we're gonna do with it. Second, yeah, because I heard somewhere that old dynamite is still good, so hopefully it will blow."

Well we met Colby's friend at the end of his driveway. He just handed us the stuff, said, "See you later" and we were on our way back to stash our new supplies up by the old car.

By the time we had done all that, it was getting dark, so we headed back to Colby's where I had planned to spend the night (Saturday night). We decided that after church tomorrow (that church without a Sunday school), and after Sunday dinner with our parents, we would head back up into the woods for our first bit of demolition.

After Sunday dinner as we headed out the door Colby's Dad asked from the living room where he and my Dad were watching a baseball game, "What're you two up to today?"

We didn't like lying to our parents, so Colby responded with, "Oh, just munging around."

Now munging around was the term we used when we had no plans, so we would just wander around until something appealed to us, then we would do it. That was munging around. The vague answer to his Dad sufficed and soothed Colby's conscience somewhat, so out the door we flew with definite plans in mind. I guess we sorta' did lie to Colby's Dad.

We hopped onto our two Hondas and headed for the old car. But not before Colby pulled an empty half-gallon milk carton from the garbage can.

Now, I need to let you know the layout of things around the old car so you can see for yourself how safe we played it even though we were playing with dynamite. Many years before, a big old fir tree had come down by the old Chevy. It lay broadside to the old car—about 20 feet from it. Its trunk was nearly 6 feet thick. This provided a perfect shelter for us. We could be only 20 feet from the blast and yet be as safe as a fox in its den. No shrapnel could ever penetrate six feet of wood! That certainty was what I tried to hold tightly to as Colby started rigging up the stuff for this particular blast.

First, he started scooping old wet dynamite powder out of the grocery bag. He had pulled open the top of the milk carton so it would hold considerably more than one half gallon. He didn't stop scooping until that milk carton was completely full. Next, Colby opened the car hood and set the milk carton on part of the engine block, after which he buried a blasting cap a couple of inches into the dynamite mush. He cut off a long length of fuse and inserted one end into the blasting cap and let the rest of the fuse drape over the front fender of the old Chevy. Finally he closed the hood and said to me, "This ought to really make some shrapnel fly." If he only knew!

When Colby approached the fuse with a burning match, I was already headed for the down-blast side of the big log.

He yelled to me, "I gave us about 45 seconds of fuse." Then he lit it.

Would it be shock and awe or just "aw shucks!"—we didn't know which.

Now both of us were tucked tightly behind the huge log. I was midway through my count down from 45 and had already planned to stick my fingers in my years somewhere around 10. Right then a thought flashed through my mind, "How many sticks of dynamite is an opened one-half gallon carton equivalent to?" I wasn't sure, but I guessed about six or seven. If it really did blow, it was not gonna be a minor explosion.

My fingers were inserted into my years. Nine, eight, seven—at about two, my head felt like somebody whopped it with a rubber mallet and simultaneously the ground shook.

At that point, Colby stood up to look. I wasn't sure it was all over yet, so I stayed put. But even though my ears were ringing a bit, I heard a whooshing sound.

Colby hollered, "Something went way up!"

I guess I really had heard a whooshing sound on the tail end of the explosion. Maybe that was what Colby caught a glimpse of. I replayed the sounds in my mind and realized that right after the explosion I had distinctly heard bits of metal spraying the bushes around us. What else had the explosion done? We went to the car to examine what old wet dynamite is capable of doing.

There were bits of metal blown away from around the engine, but the most notable change was that the hood of the old Chevy was gone—nowhere to be seen. Well, that observation prompted a search for the hood.

First we walked the area nearby searching the woods in about a 100-yard radius. No hood! Next, we both hopped on our Honda's and expanded the search area. After about two hours of fruitless searching, we gave up on the hood and headed back to Colby's place.

As we pulled up in front of his house, we saw Colby's Dad standing in the doorway. We weren't sure what to make of that, so we just waltzed in nonchalantly.

But as we entered, Colby's Mom blurted out, "What have you two been up to?"

Before we could even answer, Colby's Dad informed us that, "About two hours ago a big explosion rattled our windows. Was that you guys?"

We both were impressed to think that old dynamite could rattle the windows of a house a mile away. But Colby replied sheepishly, "We were trying to make something that would explode."

Well that was very deceptive because his Dad knew about our experimentation with saltpetre and he jumped to the conclusion that we were getting pretty good with potassium nitrate.

We never did correct Colby's Dad's erroneous assumption. That would've gotten us into a lot of trouble right when we still had one-half of a bag of old dynamite up in the woods and a whale of a lot of car yet to be blown up.

But we did correct our assumptions about dynamite. It just gets better with age. Two weeks later we stumbled across the hood of the car more than a quarter mile away in some bushes. Yes, it's hard to beat the bang for the buck that we got from our old wet dynamite.

21
Snake Charmers

Though old Nicodemus thought snakes were all evil and that they should be annihilated, Colby thought snakes were, well, charming. Their differences of opinions about snakes led to some interesting incidents, but those are best left for another story at another time.

I hated snakes, at least I hated every snake that had fangs or was poisonous. Nevertheless Colby lured me into his activities with those cursed creatures. Against my better judgment, he persuaded me to join him in becoming two snake charmers.

For any kid who grew up in rural southern Oregon, snakes were a fact of life you learned to deal with. If you had a phobia about snakes, like my Mom did and my future mother-in-law, you got a fright every third or fourth trip to the garden and virtually every time you walked through a grassy field in the summertime.

We had garter snakes in the grass and sometimes in the water. We had tons of bull snakes (those nonpoisonous but nevertheless vile things have big fangs). We had beautiful black and white king snakes which shared two things with the much more prevalent bull snakes, they both had fangs and they both killed rattlesnakes—their one redeeming quality. Then we had that most dreaded devil of a snake in North America, the rattlesnake.

Our southern Oregon timber rattlers weren't like those little sidewinders you see in the desert. These were powerful snakes, thick as a man's forearm in the middle and tapering down to a little poisonous fanged mouth on one end and on the other end tapering down to several rows of rattles that can, under enough provocation, buzz so loud that your ears would ring after a few seconds of exposure.

Before Colby and I began charming snakes, we were not on such friendly terms with them. You see, I had a knight and castle play set. We had knights with swords, knights on horseback with lances, but what we didn't have was a dragon for the knights to fight with. We quickly found a foot-long garter snake in the wet lands adjacent to my property. Now the little guy didn't want to be a dragon, so he bit me. Well, that cost him his life and he ended up being a dragon anyway.

We had great fun that afternoon making the dragon eat a bunch of knights and creating all sorts of fantasy battle scenarios. When Colby and I grew tired from two hours of nonstop conflict, we stopped and looked for something to snack on. Thinking we might get back to the knights and dragon, I coiled the little garter dragon up and dropped him in my shirt pocket—one of my best Sunday-go-to-church shirt pockets.

After our snack, Colby's parents needed to head for home, so we said our goodbyes and later that evening I hung up my Sunday shirt in the closet since I hadn't gotten it dirty, at least not by my standards of shirt dirtiness.

A funny thing happened several days later. Actually it wasn't so funny because it happened in my room. My whole room reeked of that dead animal smell that almost makes you upchuck.

We looked everywhere and couldn't find the source of the stench. Since it was late, and since Dad thought something must have crawled under our house and died, we gave up the search for the evening. I tried to sleep that night but that urge to upchuck kept me awake much of the night.

It so happened that the next day was Sunday. I put on a clean pair of pants and grabbed my best Sunday shirt, and slipped it on. I can't remember which happened first, the convulsion of my stomach from the smell or the peek I got at what was left of the decaying dragon in my shirt pocket. I do remember clearly what happened right after that—I barfed a bunch.

Well the whole story about the knights and the unwilling dragon came out, along with a little more of my breakfast, and then my Mom took the shirt to wash it, but I put up such a fuss about never wearing it again, that she finally put that shirt where belonged, in our garbage can. I slept better that night, but after church I did warn Colby about keeping dead snakes around.

Colby soon got into keeping snakes alive rather than killing them. He didn't bother with garter snakes anymore because we found out that if we caught a big bull snake, the man at the Cobra Farm (a tourist trap along Redwood Highway by O'Brien, just about a mile down the road from suicide bridge—you can read about that in another story) would pay us two dollars if the bull snake met his specifications. You see the Cobra Farm, along with their cobras, kept some rattlers and a few big feisty bull snakes.

One summer day Colby scared up a good-sized bull snake in the edge of the woods behind his house. It was a little slow when trying to get away, so Colby grabbed the snake behind its head before I could yell, "Let it go!" I yelled anyway, to no avail.

I didn't like bull snakes unless they were securely in a box on their way to the Cobra Farm. Any snake with fangs like that, over an inch long, was not charming to me and I had no wish to charm it. Colby was not a kindred spirit in this matter.

"C'mon, let me show you something," Colby urged.

Now those words usually meant something very unpleasant was gonna go down soon.

"No thanks," I said politely. "Let's just throw him in a box and take him to the Cobra Farm," was my counter suggestion.

"Sure, we'll do that in a bit," Colby said completely refusing to acknowledge my obvious angst over anything he wanted to show me involving that revolting reptile.

"Let's get in Dad's car. I can show you there."

This was getting worse by the minute—actually by the second.

"Why don't you just show me right here?"

"Can't. The car will be perfect," Colby said emphatically as he opened the car door.

A minute later there I sat beside Colby on the front seat of his Dad's blue Ford. Colby lifted the snake up, set him on the dash, and turned him loose.

My mind screamed, "You fool!" But I knew better than to scare the snake because right then he was sticking his head out toward my face. With his tongue darting in and out he let out the loudest "SSSSSSSS," I have ever heard a snake make. As my heart raced and my eyes bulged, the snake turned toward Colby and slithered across the top of the Ford's big dash until he was right in front of Colby's face where he showed his two big fangs while he coiled his body and danced side to side with his head.

Now, nose piercings weren't popular in those days unless you lived in Africa. But I was sure Colby was about to get his nose pierced in two places at once. However, Colby sat quietly and turned on his snake charm. The big bull snake relented and slithered across the dash, where he started once again giving me the hissing hysterics.

After about 15 minutes of this charming little game, I had been tortured beyond what my shot nervous system could stand, so when the bull snake wasn't looking at me, I grabbed the door handle and bailed out. Colby had made his own bed and he would have to lay in it, not me. It would serve him right if that snake gave him two more nostrils on his nose.

Colby, although he was intently charming the snake, had watched me more closely than I imagined. He had anticipated the precise moment of my abrupt departure and he seized the moment to seize the snake right behind the head again. Charm school was over. The snake went into a box where he belonged, I thought, and we went to the Cobra Farm to get paid.

When Colby held the snake out for the man to inspect, without even looking the guy said, "Don't need any more bull snakes, we've got enough."

I had spent an eternity with the devil himself hissing right in my face and now I was getting nothing as payment for my pain.

"Put that booger down, I'll take my money out of his hide!" I ordered as we exited the building. But I was too late, Colby had just tossed the big bull snake into an area of tall grass adjacent to the parking lot and the snake wisely disappeared in a flash. I started looking for a big rock to crush his big fanged, pea-brained little head. But I couldn't find a rock and I couldn't find the snake.

All Colby said was, "Charming wasn't he?"

I thought about wringing Colby's neck right then, but as it turned out I didn't need to. He was about to learn that neither bull snakes, nor Colby himself, were as charming as he thought.

A few weeks later that summer, Colby and I both climbed on the back of my Honda, and with two 22 rifles strapped on Colby's back, we headed out for an afternoon of plinking. We were going to cut through an old logging road that only a few people knew about and go to the old Chinamen's diggings. During the late 1800's gold rush, Chinese immigrants' labor had been used to dig long ditches that ran for miles. The dirt from the ditches was run through big sluice boxes to separate out the gold. Colby and I often dreamed of finding a big nugget somewhere along the ditches, that never happened, but on this day we found something else that got us pretty excited.

I was on the front, driving, and Colby was looking out on both sides for anything interesting. Just ahead I saw the head of the snake come out of the roadside grass.

I hollered "Snake!" and hit the brakes.

Colby and I watched as the head of the snake crossed most of the road and the tail had yet to emerge. When the tail finally did become visible, we were looking at the biggest bull snake we had ever seen—maybe the biggest one anyone had ever seen.

Before I could swing my leg over the Honda to get off, Colby was already running after the snake. He grabbed the fleeing snake's tail and held him up to show me that he was as long as Colby was high. The problem was the snake never let Colby exhibit his full length. The gargantuan bull snake, with one contraction of his spinal muscles, pulled his head up to Colby's hand and with amazing accuracy put his two fangs clear through the object primarily responsible for holding him in such an undignified position—that object was Colby's right index finger.

Colby hollered loudly, "Ooowww!" It was completely an involuntary response.

He then shook his hand hard two or three times to dislodge the snake that was latched onto his finger. When the big snake came loose and fell on the ground, Colby glanced at the four holes in his pointer—two on the top and two on the bottom. The site of the wounds and the pain infuriated Colby so much that he lost his charm. This snake would not be charmed, it would not be sold to the Cobra Farm, rather it died with four holes in its head from Colby's rifle.

Now Colby healed up fine—he didn't get an infection from the two piercings inflicted by those two-inch long fangs. However, this incident, to my relief, put an end to Colby's desire for us to play that game where he had deluded himself into thinking we were snake charmers.

22

The Fantastic Forward Flip

Did you ever see something so fantastically improbable that your mind just couldn't process what your optic nerve was transmitting to it? You know, something that just makes you say, "What wazzat?" One such thing, as seen by Colby and me, is what this story is about. But to tell it requires backing up in time a bit from the event itself—that event being the fantastic forward flip.

As Colby and I progressed in our swimming activities and adventures we began working on our dives. We had the art of jumping down to a science—a very finely tuned science (you can read about how we tuned our jumping artistry in another story, Suicide Bridge).

A great diving apparatus was available to us at the old swimming hole called, The Forks. The Forks, now called Forks State Park, was a popular place because you could swim in a great spot in the warm fork of the Illinois River, immediately above the confluence of the warm and cold forks of the river. The cold fork, sometimes called Sucker Creek, was about ten degrees colder and swimming there was reserved for the hottest summer days.

The Forks was so popular that some of the local men constructed a terrific diving board. They took a single long plank (a four-by-twenty-four planed pine board) and securely anchored it to the bank. It extended out about 12 feet into the river where the depth was nearly 15 feet. The board was 10 feet above the water and had tremendous spring to it. Now think about this; a hot summer day, refreshingly cool water, a great diving board and large sandy beaches on both sides of the river—what more could a boy asked for. It was paradise!

Colby learned to do a great swan dive from that board and a very good jackknife. But a forward flip, going in feet first, or a one and one-half dive, those were not his forte. A well executed forward flip became something awesome to us.

It so happened that my school had a springboard for gymnastics. My seventh grade PE teacher thought that the more agile guys (we did not have coed PE in those days) should try some stuff on the springboard. He taught me how to do a fair forward flip. I had a few rough rear-end landings. In one of those I bit my tongue so hard that I bled all over myself and the mats thus ending the class for the day. But though I had a sore tongue, I could do a fair forward flip. So I revealed it to Colby and all the other guys who were swimming at the forks one early summer day.

The guys were fascinated by this bit of acrobatics so many began trying it themselves. We saw a lot of out-of-control entries that resulted in many red water welts on sides and arms that day. Though I had mastered the forward flip (not the one and one-half dive yet), both Colby and I remained in awe of anything well executed that required one or more rotations before entering the water. We carried that sense of awe forward into our teenage years, when we saw the most awesome flip any boy could possibly imagine.

It started at the end of one of those perfect summer days of which southern Oregon's climatology is comprised. Colby and I had ridden my little Honda motorcycle to the Dairy Queen, which is on the main drag at the center of the little town of Cave Junction, a few miles from where Colby lived. We were sitting outside at a table facing the main street eating fries and drinking cherry cokes with a few other guys that Colby knew. In the background the Beach Boys were having "Fun, Fun, Fun" and the Four Seasons had just finished singing about big girls—the ones who don't cry—as the sun sank behind the mountains to the west.

Now this was before the corruption of our bubble gum music by those darned British groups. This was also the magical time of the evening where, in a boy's mind, anything could happen. Who knows, a pretty young lady might just walk right up to you and introduce herself. Or, you might see a 409 and a Stingray headed off together toward the drag strip marked out on Rockydale Road.

A magical feeling of anticipation filled the air as the long period of twilight began. We thanked the coastal mountains for that premature sunset that prolonged the magic of early evening. We also thanked those mountains for the 15 degree drop in temperature that accompanied the sunset. In addition, we thanked those mountains for the lakes they held in their Douglas-fir covered arms (but, those lakes and what we did there are another story for another time).

As we continued to sip our cherry cokes and the jukebox pounded out an endless flow of bubble gum music, it began to grow darker. The dimming of the light was so slow that it was almost imperceptible. It creeps up on a lot of people so slowly that they don't realize both how much they can no longer see and how much they are no longer seen.

About this time, a late model Chevy, obviously a kid's car, made a left hand turn into the DQ. The Chevy didn't have its lights on. The black motorcycle with two dark-clad guys on it, traveling in the opposite direction, didn't have its lights on either. About the time the two drivers first saw each other was just about the time the motorcycle slammed into the front passenger's-side fender of the Chevy.

As the Chevy began to turn into the DQ, it was right in front of where Colby and I sat, so it drew our attention. We looked up just in time to watch the entire sequence of events that ensued.

Here's what we saw. As the motorcycle's front wheel hit the Chevy, the rear part of the motorcycle came up over the handlebars and, acting like a catapult, flung the two-men into the air.

Now the motorcycle driver, being in front, was launched at a much lower trajectory. This caused him to leave an imprint of his body in the windshield of the Chevy. Unfortunately this did break his pelvis, but fortunately that was the only serious injury he sustained. It could have been much worse.

His passenger, being on the back, traveled in a much higher and longer trajectory. Suffice it to say the height of the passenger's flight would have shattered the world record high jump by at least 5 feet. The length of his flight would have shattered Bob Beamon's Mexico City Olympics long jump record (which was still 5 years in the future) by at least 10 feet. The flip he completed while in the air would have scored high in the Olympic diving or gymnastics competitions.

As we saw him rotate slowly, moving rapidly along the ark of his trajectory, it looked, well, sorta' graceful. And, best of all, he really stuck the landing. That is to say, he stayed on his feet, running down the pavement at world-class sprinter speed.

Now I was really glad, as I'm sure this fellow was, that he kept his whole body extended while airborne. This allowed him to do precisely one rotation. Had he tucked in anything, or even bent his legs, this could easily have turned into a 1 1/2 forward dive and the landing would not have been so pretty or so pain free.

The forward flipper however, did not get away unscathed. The force of the catapult ripped off both of his shoes, so when he hit the pavement on the run, he was sock-footed and sprinting with amazing speed to keep from falling on his face.

When he came to a stop about 50 yards down the street, the guy was in a daze, or a state of shock—Colby and I didn't know which. We watched him looking for his shoes while his buddy lay in pain on the street surrounded by a group of would-be good Samaritans. Shoeless Joe finally found one shoe and he carried it as he went up to one person after another asking if they had seen his other shoe. After about five minutes, this guy finally recovered his wits though, to the best of Colby's and my knowledge, he never recovered his other shoe.

As the ambulance loaded the injured man and his extremely upset wife, who had been brought to the accident scene, for the 30-mile ride over the hills to Josephine General Hospital, Colby and I replayed the scene over and over in our minds and discussed what we had witnessed. We concluded that we had really seen a man do a forward flip, flying about 10 feet above the ground after which he had landed on his feet some 35 to 40 feet from his takeoff running at nearly 30 miles per hour. Our flips from the diving board paled in comparison.

As the magical twilight time gave way to darkness, Colby and I climbed on my Honda bike making sure my head light was turned on and rode away from the DQ headed for home as Jan and Dean "busted their buns" while "Sidewalk Surfing" on the DQ jukebox.

When we began to tell other kids what we had witnessed, they eventually all believed us because our testimony was corroborated by the local radio stations who, on their news broadcasts, were also telling the story of the accident that resulted in the fantastic forward flip.

23
Bigfoot And Porcupine Pie

In 1972 Neil Diamond wrote a silly kid's song (the kind I like) about silly names given to ice-cream flavors. The flavor that the title of the song was derived from was "Porcupine Pie." I thought it was a clever title, so I have borrowed it for my own purposes. Now, the Neil Diamond song is a light-hearted, fun song, totally unlike that night when Colby, myself, and three other guys encountered Bigfoot and porcupine pie.

It all started with information from Colby's Dad that Tannen Lake had, once again, been stocked twice by mistake. So, Colby started looking for some other guys who might like to go with us and hike in to the lake for some great trout fishing. The more the merrier I thought; because we were going into the heart of Bigfoot country—I actually would have preferred a whole army.

In short order, Colby found that Dennis and Dan R wanted to come with us. They had a cousin, Rich, visiting from Southern California, the L.A. area. All three had decided to come along with us for the fishing trip.

Dan, Dennis, and Rich, packed Dan's little Willys sedan with their gear and a large cooler that we hoped to fill with pan-sized trout. Colby and I put our stuff in Dan's car too for the first leg of our trip up the mountain to Bolan Lake. Colby and I rode our Honda's up to Bolan Lake, which we bypassed for fishing purposes since the Fish and Game plane had also bypassed Bolan Lake when stocking the mountain lakes in that area. We parked the car; hid and locked our Honda's; put on our backpacks loaded with our gear, and began the four-mile hike to Tannen Lake, located in what is now the Red Buttes Wilderness in the Siskiyou Mountains less than a half-mile from the California border.

As I mentioned, the cousin, Rich, was from the L.A. area. This story takes place about the time that meteorologists were just getting the notion that the smog there was really a bad pollution problem with some nasty consequences. But it would still be many years before the pollution levels would be significantly reduced. So Rich, having lived there his entire life, had a bad set of lungs.

The first part of the four-mile hike is a steep climb to the top of the mountain—actually a saddle between Bolan Mountain and Grizzly Peak. The climb, added to the fact that we were over 5,000 feet above sea level, wreaked havoc with Rich's cardiovascular system. Now, to look at Rich you would think he was a strong 16 year-old athlete. But, to hear him hack all the way up the mountain would make you think he was a chain smoker.

Well Rich hacked and hacked. We stopped at times for him to catch his breath. The four of us raised in southern Oregon felt sorry for him, but Rich was game—he never quit. So, a bit fatigued (in Rich's case, exhausted), we arrived at the ridge to the west and above Tannen Lake, where we started our 600-foot descent down to bowl carved out of the mountainside containing the lake.

Other than Rich's coughing and sighting a big black bear, the hike had been rather uneventful, I thought, as we made camp in the only flat accessible part of the lake shore near the head of a small stream that flowed down the mountain. That little stream soon became Yeager Creek, as it flowed down to the north. Then, passing near the Oregon Caves, it would become Grayback Creek, then Sucker Creek, and finally it would flow into the Illinois River many miles below. Colby and I had fished all of those creeks and now we would fish at their source, Tannen Lake.

After a fire was going and we heated up canned foods for dinner (we would have trout for most of our other meals), we collected a pile of firewood. Then, as darkness settled in, we crawled down into our sleeping bags while the stars began their brilliant display. They were only this bright at high elevations and a long way from the light pollution of cities and towns.

As we stargazed, the coyotes began their chilling sound on the ridge almost a thousand feet above the lake. We began discussing the fact that we were almost dead center in the region where the Bigfoot sightings in Oregon and northern California had supposedly taken place. This led to the inevitable story telling.

I related to the group one of those stories that was told by a man my Dad worked with, Bud K. Bud hunted the mountains of southern Oregon for all sorts of game including bear and cougar. He hunted with this blood hounds whenever it was legal to do so—even sometimes when it wasn't. Now he told a story to just about everyone he met about crossing Bigfoot's trail.

Bud was deep in the mountains about 15 miles northeast of where we were camped when his hounds hit a trail. Bud saw some big tracks and also saw that his dogs quickly dropped off the scent—not that they had lost it; rather they chose to drop off the trail. Urge them as he might, Bud's hounds would only slouch and slink away—away from the trail. The reaction of his dogs, the tracks, and the lingering odor, convinced him that he had found Bigfoot's trail, a mere 15 miles from where we boys were camped in the heart of Bigfoot country.

Colby told another story that had spread like wildfire among all the loggers a couple of years prior. Some loggers returned to their landing in the mountains above Happy Camp early one morning to find that the landing had been trashed by something, or someone, who had superhuman strength. The biggest exploit of this creature had been to carry a 100 gallon drum about 40 yards and toss it off a cliff smashing it on the rocks below. This creature left behind huge footprints all over the logging landing.

Now the peak looming 1,000 feet above our campsite at Tannen Lake was one of those mountains above Happy Camp. That bit of knowledge spawned an extended conversation speculating on what Bigfoot was and what an encounter with him might involve. There was no speculation about the existence of Bigfoot—we had heard a preponderance of evidence supporting that—we just didn't know who, or what, he was.

"Do you think he would kill us if we ran across him up here?" Dan asked the group.

I chimed in with my logical answer, "Well, there have been a lot of sightings, but no deaths. So I'd say no, he wouldn't kill us, but I don't think we can be sure of that."

"Most of the sightings in the Northwest have been within a 20 mile radius of where we're camped," Colby contributed. "But there have been only a few sightings over a long period of time— too few for us to have much of a chance of running into him."

Right then was when the noise started. It was unlike anything Colby and I had ever heard in our years of roaming the woods and camping out. Now we had heard coyotes, cougar, wildcats, and all sorts of smaller animals, but this whumping sound of feet on the ground, the wild crashing in the brush, and the deep grunting, snorting noise really unnerved us. It especially did so since it was coming from a spot only about 50 feet from where we lay nervously in our sleeping bags.

"Colby, does that sound like a bear to you?" I queried hoping for an affirmation.

"No, they grunt like an old hog. Besides, all the bear I've seen run away from you as fast as they can—they don't hang around like this thing is doing," Colby responded dashing my hope for anything that assured me that this was not Bigfoot.

"This thing is staying right here by us—it must want something from us," Dennis added, doing nothing to reduce our level of anxiety.

Dan summed up all our thoughts in a nutshell, "I think it wants us."

Well, Dan was correct for as far as he went—in his words I mean. If he'd have added "to move" then he'd have been right on the money. We soon learned that.

You see, after Dan's blunt statement of what we all feared, we all just lay there silently in our sleeping bags trying to stay warm and safe while an unknown creature expressed its terrifying displeasure with us through stomps, snorts, and crashes in the brush that lasted for the next 15 minutes. My bed was close to the fire so I reached out and threw several chunks of wood on it. Then all grew silent. "It must be moving in for the kill," I thought.

Well, something was moving anyway. I peered through the starlit darkness off to our right. There were shadows emerging from the trees and brush, then proceeding toward the lake. I saw a doe and the largest buck I've ever seen in western Oregon.

Now the picture became clear to me and I began explaining to the rest of the guys, "Over near the logjam. See the deer? That's your bigfoot!"

"What in the heck were they doing? I've never heard deer act like that!" Colby responded.

"Look at this bowl the lake is tucked into. The only way they can get to the lake for water without tumbling down a rock slide one of the steep sides, is pretty much right through our camp," I observed quite proud of my quick analysis of the situation.

"I'm gonna' file away that snortin' sound for future reference," Colby stated emphatically. "I never knew a buck could make that sound or would be that aggressive toward people just to get to water."

I knew why Colby was so surprised. You see, he had cut down deer while camped on their water hole (that's another story for another time), but he had never cut off deer from their water hole by camping in between. The timing of the deer's protest couldn't have been better if it had been planned specifically for scaring the daylights out of us. It sounded just like something I would do to scare my little sister, Maria.

In camp there was a bit of banter as a bunch of boys released pent-up nervous energy. Then we grew tired and sleep came to all of us—that is after I threw another log on the fire.

"Yeow! Something just ran over my sleeping bag!" we heard as we were awakened in the early twilight.

That was followed by, "Yikes! It just ran over me too—I think it's a porcupine!"

"Just ran over my bag too—let's kill it," Dan yelled.

"Hey, just ran over me too—let's kill it and eat it," Colby hollered.

You see four of the guys, me excluded, had all laid out their sleeping bags in one single row—a row that became a freeway for the porcupine—a freeway that wasn't exactly free because of the toll that was exacted by Colby. Barely able to see, we all jumped up. Colby grabbed a limb that looked like a club and delivered one fatal blow to the unfortunate porcupine's skull.

Now, before you go thinking we were just a bunch of cruel kids, you gotta' understand the method behind our madness. We had been told by adults ever since we were little kids, that if you were lost in the woods and without food you, could always club a porcupine because they're so slow and that way you could get something to eat. That's all we were ever told about it. No one ever told us the rest of the story.

Colby and I had long wanted to test the porcupine proposal, but we didn't want to have to run out of food while being lost just to try it out. So, this was the perfect time, and Colby wanted to take full advantage of it. After he had taken advantage of the porcupine with that club, he popped the question that got right to the heart of the porcupine-for-food proposition "Who wants to skin this guy?"

There was no response. As I looked down at the body bristling with sharp, barbed quills I saw no place to begin without paying dearly for whatever food you might get. I remained silent with three other non-responders.

Then Colby, true to his temerarious temperament, spoke to break the silence, "Well I guess I will then."

"You can have him," I gladly conceded.

"Don't worry, I'll still share him with you guys," Colby assured us as he readied his hunting knife for the prickly task at hand.

I was grateful to Colby at the time, but that would change.

Some of the guys walked away and started rigging up their poles for fishing, but I stuck around to see Colby get stuck. You remember my thought about there being no place to begin to skin? Colby hesitated upon recognizing that, but then he just grabbed the porky, hollered, "Ow," and started skinning.

This part of the saga could well be called "porky's revenge" because even in death the porcupine exacted a huge toll from Colby's hands. Countless times I watched Colby grasp that prickly pear on legs and get a quill tip imbedded somewhere in a finger or hand. The prick was way too shallow to push the quill all the way through—the way you sometimes have to do with a dog's muzzle—so Colby just ripped out the quill, hollered "Ouch," sometimes bled a little, and continued his work.

After about an hour of torture, Colby had that mammalian cactus cut up into several hunks of meat for roasting. He then doled out our porcupine rations and left the cooking to us individually.

Rich wanted to make a stew with his portion, so he boiled his porky meat adding some salt and pepper to his brew. The rest of the guys followed my suit and roasted their porky by skewering it on a stick and then holding it over some red hot coals.

I had selected the best coals to roast my porky on so my chunk was done first. It didn't smell too bad, so sprinkling a little salt and pepper I bit in fully expecting the porky to taste like other small game that Colby and I had eaten in the wild. Well my brain kept telling me it should be good, my taste buds kept contradicting that thought in protest.

Believe it or not, my brain wanted to believe that porcupine-is-easy-food myth so badly that I had downed three or four bites before I listened to my taste buds. The story they told me went something like this—actually it was a question and answer session:

"Where do you find porcupines?"

"In the woods."

What kind of trees do you most see around porcupines?"

"Pine trees."

"What do pine trees smell like?"

"Pitch."

"What do pine trees exude?"

"Pitch."

"What do porcupines taste like?"

"Pitch!"

With that, my stomach began quivering dangerously close to hurling up the porky. After a few minutes I noticed the other guy's going silent and still. Their faces all had a greenish cast to them.

I had to either lie down or barf. I chose to lie down on my sleeping bag, where I turned on my side and tried to be still. I looked straight ahead of me as I lay there nauseous, staring a few feet ahead at a large pine tree. Near its base was a large glob of pitch that had run down and accumulated at the base of the tree. That sight was all I could take. As I jumped up, up came the pitch-flavored porky and then down I fell on my sleeping bag as my stomach continued its convulsive activity. The nausea kept me down on my sleeping bag instead of out on the lake where the trout beckoned.

Within a couple of hours we all recovered enough to do what we had come up to Tannen like to do—catch trout. Since the Fish and Game Department had stocked the lake twice, we caught a lot of fish that day.

By late afternoon, I had a lot of fish to clean, so I started looking for a place to clean them. The log jam formed by trees falling into the lake and collecting where the creek flowed out looked like a good spot. There were several logs all lined up parallel to each other, kind of like a giant raft. I walked onto the "raft" then over to its edge and, with each foot resting on one of two big adjacent logs, I went to my task of cleaning my day's limit of trout.

Just as I was finishing up my last trout, I realized for the first time that the two logs I had been standing on were drifting apart at an almost imperceptible rate. My feet were still a comfortable distance apart, so I started to push lightly on one of those logs to get onto a single log. It moved out about an inch when I applied even the slightest pressure. I shifted my attention to the other foot and the other log and pushed lightly to extract my foot from it—I got the same response. I could not shift weight to either foot without causing the logs to drift still farther apart. Next I tried contracting the muscles down the insides of my legs pulling my feet in to pull the two logs back together. While that might have worked six inches ago, it had virtually no impact where I now stood, just past the point of no return.

I hollered to the other guys for help. As things started degenerating quickly, I finally got their attention. But it seemed that their attention was focused on me and my misery only in the sense that it was just fun and games for them to watch. They watched and I hollered until, nearly doing the splits. Finally I bellowed loudly and then dropped down to my fate in Tannen Lake's version of Davy Jones' locker.

Wallet wet, cold from the icy lake, and miffed because the guys just howled in laughter at my helpless situation, I stomped into camp and began looking for dry clothes and a line to hang the wet clothes on.

Later that evening, with sweet trout meat in our bellies, and the effects of porky's revenge gone, we nestled down in our bags for a much more restful, peaceful night. As we packed out the next day, our packs iced down with glaciated snow and full of fish, I knew that both Colby and I would long remember the night of Bigfoot and porcupine pie.

24
Makin' The Grade

This story ain't about what teachers do after final exams and it ain't about what students hope they'll do on their report cards. What it's about is something that's imbedded deep in the heart of every little boy and it's about what remains there even after they become old geezers. It's what Ray Stevens so exquisitely expressed in that ditty called, "The Haircut Song," after he got that Butte Montana buzz cut—it's the desire to operate heavy equipment. Well Colby had it just like all of us guys do, so one day he decided to try his hand at makin' the grade.

After Colby's family moved to the little white house that sat on land that had once been a lumber mill, they had a driveway that was about three-eighths of a mile long. Actually most of it was shared by three other houses, so it was officially a county road and therefore, the county's responsibility to maintain.

Well the county didn't do such a hot job of taking care of the road. It got puddles in the winter that became big dips or sharp potholes by midsummer. The gravel and rock poured on it years before all went to the sides of the road and only an occasional golf-ball sized rock remained on the road, and those just caused trouble.

Colby and I raced our Honda's up and down that lumpy, bumpy road more times then we could count. One of those golf-ball sized rocks got flipped just right by Colby's rear wheel so that it went airborne and caught me on the sternum, hurting like the dickens, and causing me to rant about how the county needed to do something about the road.

Well, about a year later, Colby's driveway finally worked its way to the front of the work queue and the county road workers showed up to repair the road. Since they didn't usually pave roads that were only three-eighths of a mile long and serve only four houses, they planned just to grade the road to make it smoother, gravel it, and then roll it to pack the surface, making it firmer and much smoother.

To get all that done and still allow the folks who live there to get in and out, the county workers said they would take several days to complete their work. The supervisor of the project came and talked to Colby's Dad about parking their equipment on the front part of his property. The front part, down near the road, was flat because that's where the old sawmill had been. It wasn't being used for anything—except maybe for jackrabbits to run in at night.

Colby's Dad said, "Sure," and so one day there appeared a road grader down on the front section of Colby's property.

I was only over there once while the road grader occupied that spot, but I could sure see that the grader had caught Colby's eye. He took me down there and we walked around it in the evening after the work crew had gone home. I honestly thought this was just curiosity about how road graders were constructed and how they worked. But Colby's homework on the road grader far exceeded my limited expectations.

One evening after I'd gone back home, Colby evidently had a Butte Montana haircut moment. Unfortunately for him, he had by this time acquired enough road grader knowledge to carry out his well-conceived but ill-timed scheme. Shorting across a couple of well-exposed wires was all it took fire up the big road grader. It took a couple minutes for Colby to check out the controls— forward, reverse, throttle, down grader, up grader and then he was ready to roll.

Colby steered the big grader onto part of his actual driveway, then made the turn onto the shared driveway that was county road. As he increased the speed, his sense of power and exhilaration followed suit—that is until he heard the siren

Now Colby was almost right when he reasoned that because the little three-eighths of a mile of county road had never to his knowledge, or to Larry R's, or Ronnie K's knowledge, ever been patrolled by the county sheriff, it was a pretty safe place to take a joyride on a road grader. The reasoning was good, the odds were good, but the ethics were bad. Evidently God thought that correcting Colby's grand-theft urges before they really got him into trouble was a good thing too. So no sooner had Colby started down the road than the deputy sheriff pulled him over.

"Son, you work for the county?"

"No, but I'd like to, so I was practicing," was Colby's quick-witted reply.

"Son, you own the equipment you are practicing on?" the deputy asked, unimpressed by Colby's wit.

"No, but I would like to some day."

"Well, son, this ain't some day, it's the day I'm arresting you for grand theft. I've caught a lot of young fellows taking cars for joy rides but, I've never seen anyone take their joy ride on a road grader."

Colby was taken to the police station where they did a good job of scaring the dickens out of him. Then they called his folks and Colby, soon to be convicted felon, had to face his Dad. For him that was probably the worst part. Fortunately for Colby though, he was released into his parents' custody. He then had to appear before the judge, make his plea, and all that stuff.

On the upside, since he never lowered the blade (which would have made a real mess of things), because he really was sorry, since he pleaded guilty, and because he was still a juvenile, the judge treated Colby's crime as only a misdemeanor. Otherwise Colby might never have gotten to continue the family tradition of serving on a sub in the Navy. On the downside, for his road-grader joy ride Colby was required to do a bunch of community-service work.

Now, the next time you pass a bunch of kids in orange suits picking up trash along the highway, don't think of them as a bunch of juvenile delinquents or future felons who are gonna steal your car or your wide-screen TV. Just think of them as impulsive teens who, like Colby, were just makin' the grade.

25
Goin' For The Gold

When the competition required daring or enduring some kind of suffering, well that was Colby's domain and he pushed his luck to the limits. For some reason, in this particular feat of daring, I wanted to win even if I had to become a bit reckless. I acted completely out of character—I acted like Colby. This time it was me who was with abandon going for the gold.

I can only remember taking Colby to my special riding trail once, because we usually did our riding on Colby's side of the county. That's where most of the really fun places to ride our Hondas were located. My riding trail was an exception and Colby loved it the minute he first set eyes on it.

Now, you dirt bike riders, imagine this—you have your own private raceway running through the hills where every corner is as steeply banked as you could ever want and you can practically ride with the throttle wide open through the woods—trees and bushes flashing by in a blur. To top it all off, there is very little possibility of taking a spill. I'll bet you are wondering, "How is this possible?"

If you rode down the highway about half a mile from my house, turned off on an almost hidden trail and then turned left about a half mile into the woods, you ended up on a forested hillside looking down a stretch of abandoned irrigation ditch that ran for one and one-half miles through the woods. Now, the ditch was U-shaped, about six feet wide between its vertical sides and it was about five feet deep.

The ditch snaked its way through the hills at a very slight grade—just enough to keep the water flowing along when it was used for irrigation. When you rode the ditch you could use the side bank on the outside of a turn to keep your speed up through the turn. You could use any part of the "U" shape you needed to negotiate a turn. For the hair-pin turns you could even go clear up on the vertical sides to take them at high speeds. Of course, you pulled a few G's when you did that, but the feeling was incredible.

It was just about impossible to wreck because, as long as you stayed in the ditch, the bike was not gonna' go out from under you. Well, there was one possibility of wrecking. It was a disastrous possibility for which the consequences were so grave that you had to take extreme precaution to ensure you avoided it. Now the first time I rode the ditch, despite the euphoria from flying down the narrow trail at such a high speed, this possible calamity came to mind a short way in. It introduced itself to me as a question that arose in the back of my mind, "Suppose someone else is doing the same thing you're doing but coming from the other direction—what then?"

Now imagine this—you are doing 50 miles-per-hour near the end of a straightaway as someone on another motorcycle (bigger than yours) emerges from the turn just ahead doing 45 miles-per-hour. Contemplating a head-on collision with an impact equivalent of 95 miles-per-hour is something that just hurts deep down inside my stomach. After the collision, I imagine that when you wake up, if you wake up, there are going to be a lot of places that hurt.

That time that I took Colby up to the ditch I very carefully showed him how to eliminate that head-on collision possibility. Before you start a run from either end of the ditch, you shut off your bike and listen carefully for about three minutes (the amount of time it would take a slow poke to ride the ditch's length). If you hear any motorcycle anywhere in the vicinity, you do not ride the ditch—you just can't take that risk.

I also showed Colby about going for the record. There was this 120-degree turn where the outside edge of the ditch was a deep cut that had been made into the hillside. The bank was so high that you could round the turn as high up on the bank as you needed to make the turn at any speed up to at least 50 miles-per-hour.

Shortly after discovering the ditch trail, I noticed the big-bank turn and decided to leave my mark high on the bank. I did that and even marked my highest spot with a twig. But the next time I ran the ditch, some other rider had left a mark above mine. Well I thought, "This will never do!" So I started my run again and made a still higher mark on the bank which two other riders promptly beat. Now there was an unspoken competition to run your bike higher on the bank than anyone else.

Back to Colby's first ride—we stopped and listened. No one else was in the woods so Colby took off with strict orders from me to perform the safety check at the other end before coming back. I could hear when he shut off the engine at the other end.

When Colby rode up to me concluding his return run I asked a rhetorical question that didn't really need asking because the smile on his face said it all, "Pretty incredible isn't it?"

Then I added, "Did you go for the record on the big-bank turn?"

"Rode pretty high around it, but didn't try to take away your record," Colby said trying to disguise the regret in his voice. I figured that, knowing Colby, he would have gone for it if he hadn't been riding my bike. You could actually take a spill high up there because the hillside was all loose granite that you might slide on if you got careless. On his bike, he wouldn't have cared if he bent up something in a spill on that bank.

On my next trip up to the ditch trail I was alone and I learned something about the safe ditch trail. Even with my precautionary listening protocol, the safe ditch ain't completely safe. You see, when I shut my bike off at the beginning of the trail to listen for other riders, I was being mimicked in perfect synchronization by someone at the other end. Evidently we kick started our bikes in unison after listening exactly the same amount of time at opposite ends of the ditch trail.

I was well into my run when I accelerated out of a turn and continued accelerating down a short straightaway ahead of me when out of the next turn came a big bike—much bigger than mine.

We were on top of each other before I had fully comprehended what I was looking at. My reflexes told me to move to the right like we do when driving in the good ol' USA. Fortunately the other rider wasn't fresh from the UK, so he went up the side of the bank on his right.

Think about it for a minute. If one motorcycle rides up on the side and is laid out nearly horizontally, where is that guy's head located? It's sticking right back into the middle of the ditch. With me laying out horizontally on the opposite ditch bank, our heads were on a collision course right down the middle of the ditch. We both realized our folly at the very last second.

I tried to retract my neck like a turtle. I don't have a clue what the other guy tried. But evidently I pulled in my head just enough so that as we, for that one panic-filled moment stared into each other's bugged-out eyes and prepared for the crunching of our helmets followed by the crunching of our skulls, we passed with only a whisker to spare between them. Then we both dropped back into the bottom of the ditch and continued our rides.

I never that I know of saw that rider again, but I will never forget those eyes with the whites showing all the way around them staring into my own eyes (probably also encircled by white).

Well I had survived an improbable event and was pretty sure that lightning would not strike twice in the same place, so the next time up, I decided to really go for the record on the big banked turn—a record so high up that it would never be broken.

While I sped through the ditch heading toward the big curve, I recalled another time that I wanted a record very badly. In fact I wanted an unbeatable record. This occurred during PE in the sixth grade. I was very strong and hadn't started my adolescent growth spurt, so I weighed very little. The contest conducted by my PE teacher, Mr. Dickinson, was climbing a rope for time up to the ceiling of the gym and back to the floor. When my turn came, Mr. Dickinson said, "Go!" and started his stop watch.

With my light weight and good upper-body strength I went hand-over-hand up that rope at a sprint. Just as I was reaching out to touch the ceiling, I peeked down at the two mats on the floor, placed there as a precaution in case someone fell. Now, I had jumped from nearly this high onto soft dirt before, so two mats were no sweat for me. After touching the ceiling, I made a big circle with the thumbs and forefingers of my hands. The circle enclosed the rope without touching it—my hands would be my brakes if anything went awry on the way down. Of course, with my hands in this configuration I was no longer touching the rope. So, I just dropped to the floor—in just a fraction of a second.

"Wig!" Mr. Dickinson hollered at me, using a nickname he gave me in the fifth grade (a name which I had to endure through the eighth grade because he transferred to the junior high when I went into the seventh grade). "Wig up the middle on two!" "Wig you've got long jump, both sprints and the relay today." "Wig, fake before you pass the ball! Don't telegraph it." Although I liked Mr. Dickinson, you can see why I was glad to get into high school. Well, back to my freefall to the gym floor.

I hit the floor, absorbing most of the shock with my legs and ending up in a relaxed sitting position on the mats, with a huge smile on my face.

"What's my time?" I asked eagerly.

"Forget your time!" he yelled.

I could tell Mr. Dickinson was mad, but I didn't realize how worried he was that one of his students, namely me, might get injured.

"If you ever pull a stunt like that again, you'll flunk this class!" he threatened.

But, as he approached me, I did get a peek at his stop watch. It said just over five seconds—a full ten seconds faster than my closest competitor. That was a record that, whether Mr. Dickinson allowed it to stand or not, would not be broken.

I wanted another record that would last forever so, as I built up my speed for the turn, I entered it at breakneck speed and drifted up onto the 30-foot bank until I was nearing the highest mark (left by another biker). To get that extra assurance that my record would endure I did the only thing I could think of—I turned my front wheel directly up the bank and goosed the engine.

It doesn't take any brains to see that my impulsive maneuver was not carefully thought out. Though I was a rider with 14,000 miles under my belt, I had made a beginning hill climber's mistake. As you have probably guessed by now, I only went a little further up the hill—enough to break the record—but the maneuver also caused my bike to start that back flip thing that is the bane of all hill climbers. Realizing my mistake I fought hard to stay on. Since my little Honda only weight 125 pounds, I was able to wrestle it into submission. The nature of the submission was that the bike did a half twist in the middle of the back flip. Since I had stayed on, this left me in the unenviable position of being headed straight down the bank with the throttle wide open pointed crosswise to the ditch.

All that happened so fast that I couldn't react in time. I just remember seeing the far side of the ditch as a launching ramp that was probably gonna send me into orbit. I couldn't hit the front brake or I would lose control in the granite dirt on the bank. All I could do was hit the rear brake hard and pray.

Now, I'm not sure, but I believe God was not only smiling right then, but He was also having a good belly-shaking laugh because, you see, beyond the far side of that ditch was a thirty-foot drop off and that's where I'd be headed when I came down out of orbit on re-entry. I knew what was coming because I wasn't able to get any pressure on the rear brake until I was already half way up the far side of the ditch and headed for outer space.

It felt like I really had gone into orbit as my bike shot up the far side of the ditch and went up vertically at least 10 feet into the air. But it then fell straight back down, landing on the back wheel, its brake now locked tightly. When the back wheel hit the ground directly on top of the outside edge of the ditch, my front wheel slammed down onto the ground with a tremendous jolt. There I sat, having stuck the landing after my vault, but instead of looking at a cheering crowd, I was looking straight down the thirty-foot drop off that my front wheel sat six inches short of.

Now you can see why I thought God was laughing. He taught me a good lesson; I wasn't hurt, and the whole thing would have looked like slap stick comedy had there been an observer (there was only one in this case, Him). He even threw in the record for me just "because He could" (I borrowed that phrase from Alex Kendrick's script for <u>Facing the Giants</u>—I love that line in the movie).

On my very last ditch-trail ride, a year later, I could still see my tire marks heading straight up the bank, high above all the others—too high for anybody to beat and live to tell about it (unless, of the course, the Lord also had a lesson for them to learn).

I imagine that by this time the land around the ditch trail has been bought by some developer and there are houses all over the place up there. If so, little kids are probably riding the ditch trail on their tricycles or big wheels. Perhaps, as they grow older and graduate to 24-speed mountain bikes, they will see the marks on the bank and revive the competition of going for the gold.

26
Cancer

It started a couple of days after Colby and I had explored the hills around my house. We rarely roamed the woods there because if you went as few as two miles in you were out the other side and in someone else's backyard. At Colby's place (Uncle John's house), you could head into the woods from his backyard and walk for 60 miles without encountering civilization. But now Colby had gone home and something had gone wrong with my body.

I rubbed my hand over the lump again. It was growing fast. All the evidence pointed to the fact that I had that disease—the one that had killed every relative of mine that had ever developed this dread disease called, the big C—cancer.

As far back as I can remember I have been fascinated by books and movies about epidemics. I love to read or watch the stories about resourceful medical professionals who initially put up defenses and then mount offensives against diseases of all sorts. As I grew older, I read several Robin Cook books. What topped them all though was that movie starring Dustin Hoffman called, Outbreak. The original version was rated R, partially for language and partially for yukky stuff. Well I got my copy through Clean

Flix, a company that sold you the original plus a version that was toned down to a PG rating. They were a great little company until the RIAA litigated them out of business. But let's not get into all that right now.

Back to the subject at hand—dread diseases were fine to me as long as they were in stories—stories that did not include me as a character. I was horrified of polio after I became aware of it. But I was very thankful to Jonas Salk the day my classmates and I went through the line at school to get some of the very first polio vaccinations in the early '50s.

I had three very bad cases of the flu-like illnesses while growing up. In each case I was delirious for several days and can remember almost nothing that occurred during the heat of the battle between my immune system and those tiny little organisms that were trying to suck the life out of my body. Those little demons just move in and then start taking over cells. They were less than one millionth of my size, but three times they almost won.

Had I been clear headed during each of those battles, I would have been horrified to contemplate how sick I actually was. Now, my parents were raised believing that you don't take anybody to the doctor unless they are injured or, if sick, near death. Once I was so sick that death was knocking, but thankfully the doctor was also knocking—they did make house calls in those days. He came with a new antibiotic in hand, Terramycin, from Pfizer, to knock that nasty bug—and it did!

I prided myself to a degree in my grades, but that serious bout with the bug cost me the last six weeks of the quarter. My toughest class at the time was chemistry. I attended the first three weeks of the quarter, then missed the next six weeks, came back and took the final cold turkey. I got a C. The only C I had ever gotten in my life! That little bug had not only damaged my body, it also damaged my pride.

Now here I was with a growing lump near my lymph nodes, slightly behind my underarm. I was trying to hang on to the present, fearful of even thinking about the future. Would they try to cut it out? I didn't think that worked well if it was into your lymphatic system. If chemo existed then, we hadn't heard anything about it, so there were no such options. With the big C, it was cut or die. All too often it was cut and die anyway. Which would it be for me?

Up to this point I couldn't bring myself to look at the lump. I was just too afraid. Besides it was back just far enough that I would need a mirror to see it.

Well Colby and his folks were coming by our house later in the day. Every two weeks, when Colby's Dad got paid, they made the trip over to our side of the county where, all the super markets were, so they could stock up on groceries and other supplies. I knew that once they arrived Colby was going to see how down I was and start asking questions. Then I'd have to tell him. Though I couldn't stand the thought of it, I had to buck up and prepare to tell him. He would be the first. I hadn't personally told any of my friends or anyone else for that matter. I just couldn't talk about it, because I didn't want to even think about it. I just wanted to wish it out of existence.

I finally surrendered to the notion of bucking up and telling Colby. But then I knew he'd ask to see it. So far, I hadn't looked at it myself and I couldn't let Colby see something about me that I hadn't seen myself. So, after a few minutes of steeling myself for the coming moment, I snuck into my parents' bathroom, took my Mom's mirror back into my bedroom and shut the door. I removed my shirt and placed the mirror where it needed to be to see the growing lump. After just sitting there holding the mirror for what seemed like an eternity, I finally focused my eyes on the mirror to see the image it reflected back to me.

What I saw at first horrified and then sickened me. I was caught completely by surprise by the revelation. There, just behind my left arm pit, was the biggest bloated tick I have ever seen. He was buried in so deeply that only the hindmost part of his rear was above the skin. I had let my paranoia of terminal illnesses keep me from yanking this guy out before he could suck out half my blood, grow to the size of my thumb and bury himself in my flesh.

The first thing out of my mouth was, "Mom!"

I ran into the kitchen where my Mom was preparing a meal for us and Colby's family.

"Get it out, Mom!" I yelled.

She took a first look, and then a second, then a third look and finally replied, "I don't know how. He's just in too deep."

About that time, Colby's family drove up. I stopped my caterwauling. Almost as soon as they entered, my Mom asked Colby's Dad to take a look at my amazing misery. Now Colby's Dad was just like my Granddad in that he prided himself on how sharp he could keep his pocket knife. Both he and my Granddad could open the blade of their knife and shave the hair off their arms as cleanly as any razor blade could do it.

He said, "I can get him out," and Colby's Dad pulled out his knife.

Seeing me tense up he tried to calm me with, "This won't hurt at all—knife's too sharp for you to feel a thing."

I wasn't sure I believed that a cut by my armpit wouldn't hurt a bit, but I wanted that big bloated bloodsucking booger out. So I let him cut it out.

Colby watch curiously, but silently. I think he was just glad it wasn't him that the tick had bored into.

Colby's Dad was right, I hardly felt a thing. He made two little slits, popped out the tick slicker than a whistle and let my Mom medicate the area.

About two weeks before, when Colby and I had wandered the hills by my place, we crawled through jungles of manzanita brush which are often infested with ticks. We knew about the ticks, so we made a habit of going through a formal inspection for ticks after playing in their domain—something we had been in too big a hurry to do two weeks ago. That neglect was something I vowed never to repeat again the day I got cured from cancer.

27
The Great Sanger Peak Mountain Road Race

A mountain crag so high that it looks like it's sitting on top of the world, with a beautiful little mountain lake nestled just below the crag, plus the rush of adrenaline that comes from breaking the sense barrier on a motorcycle, followed by a freak accident, then add something so weird that a sore sight for eyes becomes a sight for sore eyes right before your very eyes, and you've got what Colby and I experienced on the day of the great Sanger Peak mountain road race.

This story starts on a beautiful late summer day with two boys debating whether or not to include a third boy in a plan to ride to the top of Sanger Peak. This third boy, Danny, was a kid that none of the other kids would have much to do with because he had some trouble with the law. But Danny had a good heart, and Colby felt sorry for him. So we invited him to join us—a decision Danny would not soon forget.

Now Danny didn't have a little Honda, instead he had a big 300-pound, bulky Cushman scooter. The Cushman had a powerful, but very low rpm, engine. However the big scooter could accelerate fairly quickly from 0 to 50 miles per hour so, all and all, Colby and I thought Danny was a compatible companion for the trip and his scooter would be compatible for traveling with Colby and me doubled up on my Honda (Colby hadn't gotten his driver's license yet).

We headed into the back country on roads so small and remote that they, in the '50s, had no name. Even today when you turn from Waldo Road, you are on a forest road that has only a number for its name. This forest road, in the '50s the locals called, Sanger Peak Road.

Sanger Peak road started in a narrow valley and then climbed the mountain for twelve twisting, winding miles—miles that became cliff-edged-without-guard-rail miles after crossing the California state line. We saw evidence of the previous wet winter in the frequent ditches eroded across the little road. The water had created either deep dips that could send you airborne or sharp bumps that would jar your teeth out if you hit them going too fast.

After we climbed up the west side of the mountain, we reached a saddle between two peaks where we crossed into California and also crossed over to the eastern side of the mountain. Here the drop-offs, some up to 1,000 feet, bordered the shoulder of the road. Once again, regardless of the narrowness of the road or the steepness of the drop-offs, there were no guardrails.

Danny and Colby concentrated on the road intently, as if filing all that road and terrain data away for future reference. That made me a little curious.

After about 45 minutes, we reached the base of the huge rock crag that was not only the top of this mountain, but also the highest point within 30 miles in any direction. Perched very strategically and magnificently on top of the rocky peak, at the 6000-foot level, was a large tower with a forestry lookout station mounted on top. Oh man, did we ever want to climb up the rock and the ladder to look out of the glass windows that wrapped clear around that station giving the occupants a 360-degree view of some of the most beautiful scenery in the Pacific Northwest. But, the big "No Trespassing" sign placed at the base of the rock by the Forestry Service, was obviously meant to prevent everyone from doing the very thing they would most want to do upon seeing the lookout tower.

Since we didn't want to get in trouble with the Forestry Service, we continued on the road for about a mile past the peak to the little bowl carved out of the mountain top where Sanger Lake lay cradled in the arms of the mountain. At first glance it was a beautiful lake that would give a fisherman the craving to cast a line into its clear waters. A closer inspection revealed that the lake was infested with black and red striped salamanders. They had choked nearly all of the life out of the lake. The salamanders were nasty tempered little demons that would bite if you tried to pick them up. They didn't have any teeth, but they could give your finger a surprisingly strong pinch.

Well, Colby, Danny and I ate the lunch we brought with us, explored the shores of the lake, caught a few salamanders, got bitten numerous times, and then finally decided that it was time to head back down the mountain.

I saw Danny and Colby discussing something so I wandered over to see what was up.

A soon as they saw me approaching Colby said, "Danny thinks he can beat us down the mountain. Let's have a race!"

Well I had seen the erosion-caused ditches crossing the road in places and I remembered well the steep drop-offs to rocks and trees a thousand feet below. Now I understood why Colby and Danny had been studying the road so carefully on the way up. They had planned this all along.

I liked doing dangerous things as long as there was a way to do them safely, so I responded with, "Do you think it's safe to do that?"

"We can race safely and sanely," was Colby's reply clearly trying to expedite this event.

Before I could raise any further objections, Danny ran to his big Cushman scooter, started it while yelling to us, "See you at the bottom!"

A bit reluctantly I hopped on my Honda and kick started it as Colby jumped on behind me while hollering, "Let's go!"

As we gained speed and started our descent my little Honda, running down hill, almost felt like a big Harley. I cranked the throttle wide open and shot by Danny at about 50 miles per hour. The rush of adrenalin took over and caution was thrown to the wind—at least for a while.

Trying to be heard over the wind rushing past our ears, I yelled to Colby, "I can take most of the ditches without slowing down if you just follow my lead! Here's a small ditch we can practice on, hang on and do what I do!"

"Gotcha!"

Now the problem with hitting ditches crosswise while going fast is that the hard bumps can either cause you to lose control of the bike or they can launch you over the handlebars. To smooth out the bump, you can brake hard as you approach the ditch causing the Honda to nearly bottom out the shocks. Then, with the shocks compressed, you quickly open the throttle all the way just a split-second before you hit the bottom of the ditch. The net effect is that you are coming up on the shocks just as the ditch is trying to compress them downward. The two opposite forces on the shocks nearly cancel one another, but you have to be sure to back off on the throttle a little just as you exit the ditch or you might go air born.

Colby, me, and the motorcycle, moved as one through the first little ditch largely smoothing it out. We stayed on the ground and in control as we crossed the ditch at 40 miles per hour. At this point, I was convinced we could take all but the deepest ditches at nearly 50 miles per hour—if I could just remember where the ditches were and identify the deep ditches while we were bearing down on them at breakneck speeds.

We passed through the next ditch fairly smoothly at 50 miles per hour. I was just getting into the idea and the thrill of, not only racing down the mountain, but also racing to win. But just then Danny shot by us on the big Cushman scooter. He was also going all-out to win and it looked like his strategy was just to run with the throttle wide open and not slow down or back off for anything.

My confidence was shaken a bit because I would not completely throw caution to the wind as Danny was doing. After all, there were several places where we would be exposed to 1000-foot drop-offs on the outside of sharp turns; then there was one really deep ditch across the road that I expected to be approaching some time very soon. I sure hoped I would recognize it quickly, because there was no way we could negotiate it at 50 miles per hour.

Right about that time we rounded a sharp turn to our right and headed down a fairly long straightaway, with Danny about 20 yards ahead of us. It appeared that Danny was going to go full throttle down the straight stretch. The problem was that I was now certain that the ditch two-thirds of the way down that straight stretch was the deep one I had been warily watching for. I started braking to a much slower speed as we approached the big bump in the road, but Danny just accelerated into it at over 50 miles per hour.

What happened next was as hysterically funny as it was terrifying. We watched Danny and the big Cushman go air born as they came up out of the big ditch. But Danny and the seat separated from the scooter, going much higher into the air than the Cushman scooter which, with the throttle still wide open, ran right out from under Danny and the seat. While remaining upright, the Cushman continued riderless down the road toward a sharp right turn with a 30-foot drop-off on the left side.

Meanwhile, Danny and the scooter seat finally came back down to earth with Danny on top of the seat bouncing and sliding down the dusty road like a cowboy riding a bucking bronco. Danny completed more than just the required eight seconds; he rode that seat until it slid to a stop some 50 yards down the road from where it first hit the ground.

All this time the Cushman scooter ran wide open straight into the turn. As the road turned out from underneath the scooter's path, the Cushman went off into the wild blue yonder. But it wasn't climbing high into the sky, it was plunging down the 30-foot bank where it crashed loudly into a jungle of manzanita bushes more than 30 feet below the road level.

I stopped my Honda as quickly as I could and Colby and I ran toward where Danny sat nearly hidden in a huge cloud of dust that his buckin' Cushman bronco-seat ride had kicked up. Through the dust we saw Danny jump up expressing two conflicting emotions, elation that he had survived his ride unscathed, and fear that his Cushman was gone forever.

The three of us scampered down to where the Cushman scooter had sailed over the bank. There was silence now—the Cushman was no longer running. But we could see part of it lodged in the tangle of manzanita more than 30 feet down the mountainside below us.

Danny laid the seat down—the one that he just ridden to glory—and started working his way down the bank, through the manzanita, to the big machine hopelessly entangled in the bushes. Danny pushed and pulled as hard as he could but, due to its weight and the manzanita, it would not budge.

After Danny climbed back up to the road, there the three of us stood on the road side looking helplessly down at the Cushman scooter manacled by the manzanita when we heard a strange racket in the distance—it was growing louder. From up above us on the mountain we heard a big four-cycle engine that sounded like it was about to go into cardiac arrest, "Putt, putt putt, pow, putt, pow, putt, putt!"

Danny exclaimed, "What in the heck is that?"

Colby and I looked up and around the corner came this—this thing. I don't really know how to describe it except to say that it appeared as if Jed and Jethro Clampett had tried to engineer their own vehicle and they were bringing the whole clan with them riding on something that only they could have created.

The contraption the Clampetts rode on was built from the frame of what once might have been a flatbed truck. They had borrowed the front end of some four-wheel drive vehicle; so, in theory, this thing had four-wheel-drive. There were no fenders or body of any sort. An engine was mounted on the front. A big old steering wheel column stuck about 4 feet up into the air where a huge wheel was attached. The driver stood on a little platform to drive the rig. Bolted onto the rear of the frame were a wooden bench (the kind you put out on your deck) and a row of three theater seats. Every seat, plus any portion of the frame that a person could successfully balance on, was occupied by a Clampett.

As the vehicle and its occupants rolled closer to Danny, Colby and me, I saw a rifle barrel poking up among the eight or nine heads. That's when I began to wonder if my characterization of these hill people was correct or not. Were we about to be written into the script for an episode of <u>The Beverly Hillbillies</u>, or into the script for the movie, <u>Deliverance</u>?

Now I know the script for <u>Deliverance</u> hadn't actually been written yet, but rumors about some places in Appalachia were in wide circulation. Outsiders were warned not to go into certain places in those mountains.

I don't mean to besmirch the character of all the Appalachian people, because many fine people live there. Who among us that are going into battle would not want to go with one of those descendants of Celtic warriors at our sides? What would America be like without the music they gave us—folk, bluegrass and country? The acoustic instruments they gave us are a delight to the ear. However, at that moment, despite what the hill people had given to America, I could not help but wonder what the three of us were about to be given—or what might be taken away.

Trying to make something good come of this, I started looking over the vehicle for Elly May. I didn't see her. Another look at Jed revealed why—Elly May just wasn't in the genes here. But I did hope there was someone like her who would at least be kindly disposed to critters like us.

After the shock of that vehicle with the Clampetts on it putt-putting around the corner at about 4 miles per hour wore off a bit, all three of our sets of eyes locked onto the device welded onto the front of the Clampett-mobile. It was a winch! But, did it work? That was the primary question. How hard could it pull was the secondary question, because to yank a 300-pound Cushman scooter free from the tangle of manzanita below and drag it 30 feet through the brush up to the road required a well-designed wench and we doubted that we were looking at one.

The driver spoke up as the vehicle eased to a stop, "You folks look like you could use a hand!"

Danny explained the accident to them. We all had a good laugh as he described the part where he went air born on the seat and then bounced and slid 50 yards down the road before stopping in a cloud of dust. The driver frowned a bit when Danny described the weight of the Cushman and pointed it out among the tangled manzanita bushes 30 feet below us.

Jed Clampett told Jethro to pull a bunch of cable from the wench, which looked like it might have 100 yards or more of cable wound up on it. Danny said he could go down and secure the cable on to the scooter.

Jed replied, "Son, I'm certain we can pull your scooter up here, but I can't guarantee that we won't bang it up along the way."

"That's O.K." Danny responded, "A banged up scooter is better than no scooter at all, and right now, that's all I've got."

"Okay, son, hook'er up and we'll have that scooter up here in a jiffy," Jed said confidently.

"We sure will!" Jethro echoed. The whole clan nodded their heads in agreement.

Those hillbillies were good for their word, and they had a fine wench, even if it did look more like an oversized deep-sea fishing reel. Shortly, the Cushman sat on the roadside. As Danny thanked the Clampetts over and over again I wondered, "Was this a God thing? Because it was just not natural."

Nothing about this was natural—the timing, the contraption, the people on it. It had to be supernatural—guardian angels or something like that. Maybe someday we'll learn who was working on our behalf—or perhaps it was on Danny's behalf.

Well, soon the Clampetts putted away on their frame-mobile and Danny began checking out the scooter. We really couldn't see any damage except for some superficial things—scratches, a bent mirror, *etc..* So, Danny straightened the mirror, set the seat back on the Cushman, swung a leg over and hit the starter. The Cushman wouldn't start! He tried until the battery went dead. We then gave up on that idea and formulated another plan.

First, Colby and I declared Danny the winner of the great Sanger Peak mountain road race, because he was ahead when the yellow flag came out and this race was definitely going to finish under the yellow flag. Danny sat on the big old Cushman and used its weight to good advantage. It coasted all the way down the mountain to the county road as Colby and I rode along in second place making sure Danny didn't have any problems.

Now Colby and I had no problem conceding the race to Danny. After all, anybody that would attack the big ditch at better than 50 miles per hour surely would have beaten us had they been able to continue. Not even the thousand-foot drop offs had slowed Danny down.

Once we reached the county road, Colby and I rode to the nearest phone and called one of Danny's relatives to pick up him and the Cushman scooter.

After that day, Colby and I didn't have any opportunities to hang out with Danny. We never knew if he got the Cushman to run again. I hope Danny was able to keep himself out of trouble and I hope the time we spent with him helped him realize that there are good, sane, and angelic kids like Colby and me that he can hang out with and have lots of clean fun and weird experiences like the three of us had on the day Danny won the great Sanger Peak mountain road race.

28
The Christmas Gift
For Anybody

The gift Colby and I gave had to be really special. Its contents were carefully selected and the package carefully wrapped because this had to be a Christmas gift for anybody.

It was a short time before Christmas in the year that we elected a young president who would not serve his entire first term. Of course, Colby and I could not peer into the future and see the events that would unfold shortly in our nation. But, on a lighter note, we did try to peer into the future and see the unfolding of our plan and we laughed at what we saw with each attempt at clairvoyance. Our laughter was not snickers or chuckles; it was a series of great belly-shaking guffaws reserved for only those times when our chicanery results in a joke, with mega mirth and a touch of treachery in the trickery—a giant joke played on someone else.

Now Colby had gotten the idea for the prank from the story told about one of his uncles who had pulled it on a neighbor. The victim in our planned prank was anybody. Only time would tell us who.

This would not be our first prank pulled on a random victim. I think I have mentioned before that my house was near a golf course. Consequently, I had an endless supply of balls from the slices of countless duffers with high handicaps.

All of the golf balls of that day and time were constructed of what seemed to be miles of thin, rubber band-like material. One Halloween, I wove a giant spider web over the entry to our front porch using golf ball rubber bands. Needless to say, we had no trick-or-treaters that year—it would have taken a knife to get through the maze of rubber. Mom was mad when she saw the monstrous web.

Colby and I thought it would be really startling if you were a driver on a country road and suddenly you thought you saw a wire stretched across the road about to hit your windshield. Of course we just stretched those ultra thin strips of rubber from a golf ball across the road, but they sure looked like a wire as they became visible through the windshield just before the car silently and harmlessly snapped the fragile rubber bands.

We saw everything from rapid slowdowns to panic stops as our rubber bands popped on impact with windshields. If the driver got out, all the evidence was gone because the broken rubber band snapped back and ended up as two very short pieces of rubber well back into the bushes on each side of the road. Even drivers that got out never found any evidence of what had hit their windshields. Fortunately no one was hurt in the panic stops. All in all, it was a stupid thing for us to have done.

Our current plan did not involve golf balls and it was tailored to the Christmas season. Since the time was about two weeks before Christmas, Colby thought our approach made our deception more, well, deceiving.

Here's what we did. Colby found a heavy cardboard box that was just the right size to hold a basketball. But rather than put in a ball, we headed for a neighbor's place to get the contents.

"Mr. Hubbard, can we shovel your barn for you?" was Colby's approach.

"Sure, right nice of you boys to do that."

"We want to take a few scoops for fertilizer when we're done. Is that OK?" Colby asked.

"Take all you want, son. My manure pile is starting to run over a bit anyway."

After considerable work shoveling out the barn, Colby grabbed our box and, with the shovel in the other hand, started carefully working his way around the muck to the absolutely muckiest part of the barn yard.

"Hope those aren't your good tennis shoes," I said fully realizing that one slip by Colby and the shoes would have to be tossed.

I don't know what Mr. Hubbard had been feeding his cows, but evidently it was making them really loose—cows tend to be a little bit that way even on good grass and good hay.

"Don't worry. This is as far as I'm going. See the really fresh green stuff? Colby said pointing with the shovel to some of the loosest of the fresh deposits.

"See it! I can smell it from clear over here. You sure the box will hold it without coming apart? It's gonna be in there for a while you know," I commented all the time thinking, "No way I'm gonna carry that box around. It's liable to fall apart right into your arms and then—" well I just couldn't let there be a "then."

"Got all that under control," Colby stated confidently.

If he was that confident the manure would stay in the box then I'd let him carry the doggoned thing—or was it a cowgone thing?

Well, Colby deftly scooped three shovelfuls of the most nauseating runny green stuff into the box.

"Don't worry," Colby said trying to assure me, "I lined the inside of the box with plastic. It'll keep the stuff and its smell where it belongs until the right time."

When we got home, Colby's shoes had survived and so had the box—so far anyway. So we sealed it really well with duct tape.

Next we wrapped the box carefully in two layers of the most elegant Christmas wrapping paper we could find. For the final touch, we put on a big bow held on with ribbons that went around the box.

"We need to put this thing right on the shoulder of the road. People will think somebody's Christmas package fell out. It's best that we don't put one of those "from-to" stickers on it or somebody might try to find who it belongs to. We want them to have no reservation about opening it right on the spot," Colby explained indicating how thoroughly he had thought through this prank.

But having some of my own concerns, I suggested, "We gotta' hide this where we can watch from behind bushes—somewhere we can be really close to see the fun. But we need to have a way to escape so we can't be followed, 'cause some people may really not appreciate this gift."

"We gotta' leave it where there is an easy spot to pull off the road right by the package," Colby added thus completing our specification of our drop-off spot.

I thought that the shoulder of the road below the big bank along the Oregon Caves highway by the turnoff to the old swimming hole would be perfect. It met all of the requirements. We could hide in the thick bushes above the bank and could run straight back into a forested area to a spot near Cemetery Road, where we could hide our bicycles. We'd be home free if anyone got so mad they chased us.

"You realize that those bushes are only twenty-five or thirty feet from where the package will be? We'll have to be quiet as mice," Colby emphasized.

We agreed on all that, so Colby tied the package onto his bike and we pedaled our bicycles to the designated hiding place and then slunk through the woods to the Caves Highway edge.

"Any cars coming," Colby asked me with his arms wrapped around the gift.

I still hadn't touched that package since we got it wrapped. "What if the plastic in the box sprung a leak?" I thought to myself.

I said there we're no cars in sight, so Colby made a quick scamper down the bank, placed the beautifully wrapped package on the shoulder of the road, just barely touching the pavement, and sprinted up the bank back into the bushes.

Being so close to the victim and having such a bird's eye view of everything was going to make keeping silent the hardest part of this whole prank. When the first car appeared in the distance, I started laughing as I pictured the surprised victim—I just couldn't stop.

"You'd better keep quiet," Colby warned, "If the wrong person gets this they just might be able to run us down—if they're mad enough."

He was right. Depending on the victim's temperament, athletic ability, strength of their desire for justice and desire to kill us, that could happen. As the car slowed down, my laughing did not. I couldn't stop even if it killed me—and it just might.

But the car accelerated again as the driver passed on the free Christmas gift that came with a price. But still a loud snicker came out of my nose and mouth.

"Keep it down! The funny stuff hasn't started yet. You can laugh while we're running through the woods," Colby said becoming a little aggravated at me for my laughing incontinence.

You see, Colby could control his laughter, if not his emotions, a little better than me.

Well a second car's driver also passed on the pernicious present. Then a logging truck running empty appeared speeding down the highway at well above the speed limit. No surprise—that's how all loggers drive. The logger hit the brakes hard as the package became recognizable and he started pulling over to the side of the road.

"This is it!" Colby exclaimed in a muffled holler. "You better keep it quiet. You know how loggers are. That stuff in the box, well some of them might try to beat it out of us," he added just adding to my angst about a possible snickering snafu.

Still seventy yards or so away the driver hit the gas pedal and accelerated as fast as an empty rig can accelerate.

"Hey, man, what's he up to now?" Colby said sounding somewhat alarmed.

At the last second the logger turned the steering wheel to line up his right front tire with the Christmas package. Then he hit the package at a speed that sent green manure flying all over the road, the front of his truck, and his windshield.

"No way!" I yelled in disappointed protest.

But he kept on flying down the road until his big rig was out of sight and our prank had gone the way of our package's contents.

No longer was I biting my tongue to keep from laughing. All that work, the beautifully wrapped package, scooping the manure from the freshest part of the barnyard—everything had been for naught. In the end, the joke was on us, and a Christmas gift for anybody had become a Christmas gift for nobody.

29
Cliffhanger Beyond The Blowhole

A huge coastal rock that juts one-quarter mile into the ocean can contain enough mysteries to keep a couple of boys occupied for a whole day—especially when the tide traps them there. The blowhole discovered by Colby and me was fascinating, but we could have done without the cliff hanger beyond the blowhole.

The southern Oregon and northern California coasts were cool and cloudy most of the time. The ocean water along these coasts was pretty cold because the current produced something called upwelling. A short translation for the non-oceanographer and non-meteorologist is that the current accelerated causing cold water to be drawn up from below—you know, the law of the conservation of matter was at work.

The coast was scenic, rugged and beautiful, but it was cursed with the impact of relatively cold sea-surface temperatures that lead to a lot of fog and low clouds. Once in a while, the curse is temporarily broken by something called off-shore flow. When this occurs, katabatic (down slope) winds warm and dry the air as they blow down the coastal mountains to the sea.

Off-shore flow occurs occasionally at Brookings, Oregon, and when it does, skies turn sunny and blue. High temperatures sometimes reach ninety degrees right on the beach during summer and early fall. This turns the cloudy, dreary coast into a paradise.

Well, my family was vacationing for a week on the coast near Brookings and they let me bring along Colby. At this time a stationary high had parked inland and it gave Colby and me seven days of off-shore flow—seven days of paradise on the beach.

Back in the '50s Mill Beach in Brookings was a little-known beach. Actually it was two adjacent beaches both wonderfully sheltered from the rough sea. We planned to spend the entire day there. Now Mill Beach had a huge rock a least 100 feet high that extended nearly a quarter mile out into the ocean. At low tide you could dodge the waves and scamper out onto this rock. Colby and I had done that numerous times to fish off the south side of the rock where the water was about 20 feet deep and, in the '50s, teeming with fish.

Two things Colby and I had never done were first, to go all the way around the rock to explore its mysteries and second, to climb onto the top of the flat-topped rock to see the view. We had arrived early in the morning, near low tide, so this seemed like the perfect day to do both of those things—we had plenty of time. So off we went running out onto the rock between waves, then climbing around the side of the rock where we had fished, and finally going beyond to where we had never been.

"Hurry up, Colby! You've got to climb through this low spot in between the waves or you'll get wet or get knocked off the rock," I yelled in impatiently. "We're almost around the corner where we can see what's on the outer end."

Colby zipped through the low spot in between the swells, and then scampered up the rock beside me as I had climbed up about 30 feet above him. Climbing around at the 30-foot level looked to be the easiest way to get to the end of the rock.

"You think we'll find a better fishing hole out there?" Colby asked with a hopeful sound to his voice.

I was just rounding the corner and getting a first glimpse of the seaward part of the rock.

"Well, I would've bet on it, but I'd have been wrong. There's only a bunch of rocks, no deep water, lots of rough water, lots of seaweed—basically just a lot of places where you can get your line hung up."

Colby rounded the corner then looked seaward with a disappointed expression.

"C'mon, let's see if there's anything interesting out here," he said perking up a bit as he stood to go further around the end of the rock.

Just then we both heard a deep rumble somewhere inside of the mammoth rock. A few seconds later, a little higher up and further around toward the end, we heard a hissing noise like when you pull the air hose off from your inflated bicycle tire. That was immediately followed by a jet of water shooting high into the air—nearly as high as the rock itself.

"Did you see that?" I exclaimed.

But by the time I got the words out, Colby was already scrambling over to the point where the hissing sound and the geyser-like column of water had come from.

When I caught up to Colby he was standing on a rock bench looking at a five-foot wide split in the rock—it had an identical rock bench on the other side of the gap.

I started to speak, but Colby hushed me up very quickly, "Shhhhh! Listen."

Then I heard it too—a deep rumble much like a very long peal of thunder.

"Cool ma—", I almost got my words out before I was drowned out by an earsplitting "Pshhhh" accompanied by a blast of water shooting 60 feet up into the air from between the two rock benches.

Both of us jumped quickly backward, partly because of the noise and partly because we were in awe of the sheer force of that jet of water.

"How often do you think it does that?" Colby asked, not really expecting an answer as much as he was hoping he could see a few more water blasts.

"Let's see," I responded turning the back of my left wrist up and focusing my eyes on the second-hand of my watch. Observe, measure, predict—a progression I was destined to make a living doing a dozen years later—I hadn't a clue about that yet even though I was performing that progression right then.

As I stood beside Colby on the rock bench timing the interval between geyser-like eruptions, we heard another long, deep, ominous-sounding rumble lasting about four seconds. A second or two later, the geyser shot up just inches in front of us.

"Six seconds," I informed Colby, and then added, "But I might have missed a second or two before I started timing."

The rumble had just concluded when another jet of water shot skyward.

"Between seven and eight seconds that time."

Colby then expressed exactly what I was thinking, "Just like Old Faithful!"

We timed a few more eruptions of "Old Faithful" and found there was a little variation, but seven to eight seconds appeared to be the average time.

"You know I heard somewhere that the average interval between ocean swells is seven seconds all around the world—sort of like the cadence of God's earth song," I said feeling proud that I was waxing so eloquent.

"Right, Longfellow," Colby quipped.

"You bet it's right and I'll prove it," I proclaimed emphatically as I stepped to the edge of the bench we were on and struck the standing long jump pose.

Colby shrunk back with anxiety showing on his face. I knew the source of it. You see, for all his reckless daring, sometimes he exhibited a fear of heights. I never knew for sure when he would have that fear, but I had learned to recognize its presence in Colby's demeanor and I was seeing it now. So, I made an appeal to that unspoken code of boyhood honor to help him overcome his fear—he had done that for me often enough, so I felt obligated to return the favor.

"I'm gonna jump across to the other rock. Watch. I'll wait three and one-half seconds after the next spurt and then jump—it's perfectly safe," I said trying to sound like a combination of a Ph.D. oceanographer and Clark Kent.

I jumped over the five-foot crevice in the rock at the appointed time, landing easily and quite safely on the other side. It had the desired effect on Colby. No way was he not going to jump over that 40-foot deep crack in the rock after I had challenged him.

"Time it," he commanded.

"One, two, three, jump!"

Colby sailed across easily and safely.

Now I had timed even more swells then Colby was aware of, so I came up with another challenge.

"Watch this," this time it was me doing the commanding.

"One, two, three, four, five," on six I jumped and Old Faithful blew almost dampening or destroying my buns—we didn't know which. Not knowing bothered me. How strong was the blast of water? I needed to know; heck, if we were gonna start playing chicken with a blowhole we both needed to know.

To get some more empirical data I stuck my arm out well over the crevice and said, "Colby, watch this."

As the next blow of the blowhole shot up, my hand felt like one of those disciplinarian-type teachers from the nineteenth century had slapped my hand with her ruler for punishment.

"Yikes! It's pretty strong!" I yelped with pain and surprise in my voice.

"I don't think we can afford to let it hit our bodies when we're jumping across—it might take us with it—off the rock and down there," I said pointing down through the crack to a big cave opening 40 feet below us at sea level.

"Watch this," Colby said catching me by surprise as he jumped at the last possible fraction of a second.

I noticed that his rear end was a little wet when he landed on the other side.

Colby had solved the mystery of our newly discovered blowhole and, from his own analysis, had used a more accurate timing approach so he could really cut his jumps close. Now that was vintage Colby! Then he explained to me what he thought was going on down below and far back into that big rock.

"The top of the mouth of the cave is right below our feet and it angles down toward sea level as it goes back into the rock. The sides must angle in too so that the cave is pretty small where it ends back inside of this rock. When a swell comes in all the water gets compressed until it has nowhere to go—"

"But right up here," I interrupted and pointed at the next expulsion of water.

"But how did you time that last jump so close?"

"Well, I've been counting time from the end of the rumble to the jet blast—much more accurate," Colby answered proudly.

He had been doing the old, "One, one thousand, two, one thousand," method of counting seconds. From the end of the rumble, he only needed to count two seconds—that never varied.

His discovery spawned nearly two hours of fun things to do with a blowhole. We put just about everything in the blast but our own bodies, though Colby came pretty close to putting his own in a couple of times. Finally, wet from the spray and tired from all the play, I climbed around the edge of the rock to look back at the way we had come on our way out.

We were completely cut off by the tide if we tried to backtrack to get off the rock. We had three options, wait six hours for a lower tide, try to climb over the rock, or try to go around the unexplored far side of the rock to get back to shore. I figured the quickest way out was to climb right up to the top and walk the flat top back to shore to get off. We already knew the rock was climbable on the beach side—I was about to try the seaward side. As Colby lingered I started up the rock. The climbing looked easy as there were plenty of foot and hand holds. That ended when I got within 25 feet or so of the top. The rock there was very smooth so, at that point, I backed down.

Even before I was all the way down to the blowhole Colby hollered, "Let's explore the rest of the rock," and headed around the end of the rock to the unexplored north side—the side I hoped would take us back to shore.

On the way we dropped down closer to water level and peered into holes between the rocks. We saw twenty-legged starfish, big purple spine-covered sea urchins, and some strange looking fish. But to proceed, we had to climb up the rock a ways. At about 40 feet above the water we were blocked by a spine (or hog back) that ran down from the top of the rock nearly to the water.

Colby somehow concluded that he could climb to the top of the rock if he could move about 60 feet to our right. I had a better vantage point than him and saw his path ending on the face of a sheer cliff with no handholds or foot holds. Furthermore, the rock looked real shale-like on that cliff face—the kind of stuff that just breaks off when you grab it.

I yelled, "Colby, stop! You'll only get trapped out there!" because that path only led to a dangerous dead-end. But, he was determined to keep going.

Before I could yell again, Colby moved out on to the dangerous part of the cliff face where there was nothing to hang onto and the rock was mostly the brittle shale stuff. I dared not yell or talk at all. Colby was starting to struggle and needed his complete concentration at this time.

I stared at the jagged rocks 40 feet below Colby, right at water level. That was his only recourse if he chose to jump, or his only landing spot if he fell. There was no friendly pool of water that he could bail out and land in.

Just then Colby's left handhold, one of those shale-like rocks, broke off. Then his right handhold broke loose too. He was spread-eagled against the sheer cliff wall. He had nothing to hold on to, so he began grabbing one hand hold after another. They each broke off—one hand hold after another.

Colby began clawing like a madman, trying to grab anything stable but without success. Then he started teetering like a person who has lost their balance and has just gone beyond the point of no return—just beginning their fall.

I was too scared and my eyes locked too tightly on Colby to even think of something like praying. As his body tilted away from the rock face to begin his plunge downward, he threw out his hand that was closest to the rock and grabbed for something—for anything. Well his hand grabbed something. I couldn't tell what he had his hand on, but at least it hadn't broken yet. However his body still leaned outward from the rock, ready to fall at any second.

Colby pulled himself back into the rock as quickly as he dared using his one good hand hold. Back against the rock, he placed the hand without the hold flat against the rock and just stood there shaking. Colby shook for several minutes—several minutes that seemed like an eternity to me.

When he stopped shaking, he began inching back toward me very, very slowly, making sure of every hold before placing any trust in it. It looked like he might make it—at least that's what I chose to believe.

I gasped loudly and started sucking in air as fast as I could—I hadn't been breathing for I don't know how long—maybe for a minute or two.

Two minutes ago, I wouldn't have bet a plug nickel on Colby's life and there was no way I could have tried to risk my life to save his—it was the ultimate helpless feeling. Now that Colby was nearly out of danger, I began to look for some safe alternate way off the rock. And if I couldn't spot one, I was determined to wait out the tide even though my parents might be in a state of panic before we made it back. We at least would be safe if we did that.

It took Colby forever to inch his way off the face of the cliff. Near the end of that "eternity", a movement caught my eye off to my left, near that blocking hog back. I watched a squirrel run right up the spine of the hog back clear to the top of the rock.

As Colby stopped beside me to recoup from the ordeal, I told him to wait there for a minute while I checked something out. At that point he was very content to just sit there for a while and I'm guessing he was sending some thanks heavenward.

I scampered over to the trail the squirrel had taken and was amazed that there had been something like an optical allusion from where I sat that made the squirrel trail look like a razor-thin spine. As I got closer, it became clear that the hog back was at least a foot wide and was certainly climbable if not walkable.

When I finally coaxed Colby over to see the trail and we started walking up the big rock, we didn't even have to use our hands. We just walked all the way to the top of the rock.

On top, there was an area of grass and dirt near the outer end of the rock. We sat on the grass enjoying the magnificent vista for a while before we walked off the rock. Not one word was spoken of Colby's cliffhanger that day. We never spoke of it again. It's life-ending potential was not something we wanted to contemplate and, as far as I know, have not until, as an old geezer, far closer to the end of my time on earth than the beginning, I can tell the story with a better perspective. Having done that, I am now truly thankful for the many years that God gave Colby and me to share after that cliff hanger beyond the blowhole.

30
Suspended Animation

It seemed like everywhere you looked in the science-fiction domain of the '50s you saw references to it. All the great science fiction writers talked about and used it in their books. Colby and I even saw it on TV. We wanted to see for ourselves if it was fact or fiction and, since we had done many other things to grasshoppers, why not try a little suspended animation?

When Colby and I were really young, his big sister, A.J., sometimes played Flash Gordon with us in our spaceship up in the attic of their woodshed. We had a control panel made of old radio parts and anything else that seemed appropriate to attach to the one by ten board that we used. We took long space flights and sometimes needed suspended animation to survive them. As we grew older we read Asimov and Heinlein's stories about suspended animation.

Suspended animation was sure a hot topic in science fiction of the '50s and '60s. Colby and I viewed it as a possibility, but in order to become real believers, we wanted to see it happen for real. For Colby, he wanted to see it happen because he had made it happen—that was Colby.

Well we discussed how to go about taking a living organism down to near death, holding it at nearly the same age, and then reviving it. Since most writers used some sort of freezing or super-cooling to perform it, Colby and I decided to freeze a living organism.

We looked around for a likely species to try. We had ruled out the cat, because Colby's Mom would have a cow if she found a cat in the deep freeze. We had to try something of little value, so pets were off-limits.

Colby thought it would be great if we froze something in an ice cube, so we limited our search to something small. It was in the middle of summer and there were grasshoppers everywhere. They met the size criterion and having caught, tried and hung them many times (you can read about that in another story), we had a lot of experience with grasshoppers. So, grasshoppers it would be!

We found an unused ice cube tray and borrowed it. We filled it with water, caught the biggest hopper we could find, took everything out to the deep freeze in Colby's Dad's shop and stuck the hopper in a cube of the ice cube tray placing a board on top to make sure he couldn't hop out. Colby slammed the freezer lid and we waited.

Now we didn't want our experiment to just look like it was suspended animation—we wanted the real thing, so we defined some criteria that had to be met for real suspended animation. The main one was that the hopper had to remain frozen for many times the length of time it took for one to die. So we drowned some grasshoppers and found that after one hour underwater they were definitely dead. Based on that, we reasoned that if we could revive a grasshopper that had been completely frozen for at least three days, that would be real suspended animation.

About that preserving the age part—we hadn't a clue how to test if the hopper aged or not. So, even if the emotional stress of the freezing ordeal aged the hopper greatly, as long as he revived after three days, that was good enough for us.

Well after three days of impatiently waiting, we popped the cubes from the ice tray and put the one with the hopper in it out in the sun to thaw. We even did a little artificial respiration (CPR had not been invented yet) by massaging the bug's thorax. It wasn't any use—he was deader than a doornail.

Since our approach was pretty crude, we thought we may have to try several times to get it to work. So we caught another big hopper and ran the experiment again. Same result! Repeatability—once you have achieved that in an experiment, you have either verified or disproven your hypothesis according to the scientific method. We tried twice more and couldn't get any of those big hoppers to revive. We were about to conclude that we had disproved suspended animation..

When I was about ready to give up on the whole idea and render suspended animation forever in the domain of science fiction, Colby suggested one last thing, "Let's try it on a really young grasshopper."

Now I wasn't an entomologist. I didn't know that grasshoppers can survive freezing temperatures as eggs or nymphs, or that even a few species can survive freezing as adults. I don't know how those hoppers survive, whether by getting rid of cellular water so freezing doesn't kill them, or by making themselves some kind of cellular antifreeze; but, by picking a young hopper, we were unknowingly getting closer to something that might work. At least we were finding a hopper that freezing by itself might not kill.

After Colby and I froze the young grasshopper we promptly forgot about him and got caught up in all the swimming and fishing that are available in the summertime. About a week later, Colby opened the freezer to get something for his Mom and saw the ice cube tray. He grabbed that ice tray from the deep freeze and we began slowly thawing the young grasshopper in the warm sun.

As his body emerged from the receding ice, he didn't look so—well, he didn't look as dead as the other grasshoppers had. Colby tuned right in on that development. He rolled the little guy over and gently massaged his abdomen and thorax, trying to get some air to move through those breathing holes called spiracles. We had watched live hopper's abdomens go in and out and figured that must be their breathing. We just needed to restart it for this little guy.

As Colby grew tired of massaging the grasshopper and finally stopped, the little abdomen kept moving in and out by itself. Pretty soon the hopper flipped himself over and hopped slowly away. All this happened after seven days in a deep freeze! That certainly met our criterion for the real thing. But despite that, I can remember asking myself as the little hopper feebly hopped away, "Have we only succeeded in injuring a grasshopper, or really accomplished suspended animation?"

I didn't know the answer to that, but one thing I did know—trying them and hanging them was a lot more fun than suspended animation!

31
The Ones That Got Away

To be sure, among anglers tall tales about long fish are widely proclaimed. Considering how, when, and where Colby and I caught ours—well, it just made matters worse. There was no way in heck anybody was gonna believe our story about the ones that got away.

I grew up in southern Oregon where my Grandpa was the fishing head of a fishing clan. When I was still a little squirt, he taught me all the good stuff fisherman need to know, like where to dig for worms, how the pick a good worm, how to rig up my line, how to bait a hook, how to cast—oh yeah, and how to hold my mouth. He kept me busy trying to learn that mouth thing for months.

Now it was two or three years before I learned that you can hold your mouth any doggone way you please. The fish just don't give a hoot. But for two or three years I worked on holding my mouth just right, and for two or three years Grandpa was the jolliest fisherman I knew. He was always laughing about something. Eventually I learned he was laughing at all the silly faces that he conned me into making, like the suck-your-cheeks-into-your-mouth fish face.

One day the laughing stopped for a bit; that happened the first time I out fished Grandpa. It wouldn't have been quite so bad if I had just caught more fish than him, but the way it happened just got his goat.

We were trolling a mountain lake for trout using ford fenders and lures. We were both catching trout, but then I started catching catfish too—one right after another with ford fenders and a little red and silver lure called a "super duper." You're only supposed to catch those sharp-finned things on bait lowered down to the bottom of the lake.

Grandpa just shook his head in puzzlement and finally shrugged in resignation as I reeled in one catfish after another. He didn't start laughing again until we got back to camp and he started telling the story of me and my catfish to the rest of the clan. I think he made it into one of his tall tales and told everyone that we had some special bait that made catfish go so crazy that they thought they were trout.

Colby, on the other hand, learned the art of fishing seat-of-the-pants after he got a spinning reel outfit for his ninth birthday. That's when we really got into fishing—together.

In the '50s southern Oregon was a fisherman's paradise. We had the famous Rogue River and its tributaries for steelhead, salmon, trout (and occasionally suckers—I just cut my line rather than touch one of those gross, big-lipped, bottom feeders). There were numerous mountain streams that you could fish downstream from hole to hole sneaking up on the big ones lurking there (I just loved that kind of fishing). We had low lakes with both trout and warm water fish like bass, bluegill, and crappie (don't blame me for the spelling—some Americans in the 1800's decided to spell it like that). Then we had beautiful, high mountain lakes that you could hike into and have a whole lake to yourself to catch rainbow trout and sometimes brook trout. Finally, we had the Pacific Ocean, where you could take your pick of surf fishing, casting into a deep hole off one of the numerous big rocks, or chartering a boat and either bottom fishing or going after salmon.

It so happened that Colby's Dad worked with a fellow whose brother worked at the local Fish and Game office. That connection permitted Colby and me to keep up-to-date on all the fish-stocking activity. We knew when, where, and with what size fish, each river and lake in our area was stocked. Better yet, we heard about all the foul-ups, like the time one isolated mountain lake (mountain lakes get stocked by air drops) was mistaken for its twin, a few miles away, and got stocked twice. When Colby and I heard about that, we made a beeline for that lake where the fishing action was nonstop. That's also where there was some "bigfoot" action, but that's another story for another time.

The incident I really wanted to tell you about happened on one of those hot, late July days, down in the valley when trout fishing is at its worst. You either can't find them, or they're just not biting, or both. So even the experienced fishermen just stopped fishing the rivers for a couple of months. Well, that's not quite true. A lot of them still would put in their time at the river. They knew in advance they wouldn't catch anything, but it beat mowing the lawn, so they just didn't tell their wives what they knew.

Well, Colby and I had a hankering to feel the tug of a trout and see the splashing of a big rainbow as it danced on the water. Despite the date and the weather, we started preparing for the two and one-half mile bike ride to the lower part of the cold fork of the Illinois River (sometimes called Sucker Creek, or the east Fork). We thought this stream would be our best bet for catching trout at such an unlikely time.

For bait, Colby thought worms and I thought eggs. We concluded a passionate debate by digging some worms, bringing our eggs and, of course, an assortment of spinners (including my catfish-catching super duper, which I always took with me for good luck).

Fishing at noon in one-hundred degree weather in late July was going to be a severe test of our angling skills. But we had a trick or two up our sleeves and we knew if we could pull this off somehow, we would be the talk of the valley. I knew my Grandpa could be relied on to spread the story of our exploits, albeit in a greatly exaggerated form, all over the county.

Now Colby and I knew about a deep channel between an island and a shady river bank. To the best of our knowledge, no one had ever fished this stretch of river because it was nearly inaccessible.

If you approached this channel from the river bank side, the first obstacle was 50 yards of dense, waist-high poison oak. That would stop most people dead in their tracks. But the poison oak alone wouldn't stop Colby and me because we both had acquired immunity to poison oak's irritating toxins.

For the non-immune, that stuff can make you itch like duck down tickle torture with Colby at the feather (you can read about that in another story). But, with poison oak, despite your scratching, the itch just keeps on going for days. In fact you can scratch 'til you bleed (many people do this) but that just spreads the toxin and greatly prolongs the misery.

My poison oak immunity was acquired at an early age while playing cowboys and Indians with two of my cousins. As we rolled all over the ground in deadly hand-to-hand combat, we unknowingly were rolling in a patch of poison oak. We were just having too much fun to notice the danger. But I noticed it immediately upon awakening the next morning.

As I opened my eyes that morning I couldn't see, that is unless you call peering out of two one-eighth inch slits, seeing. I peeked through the slits into a mirror and saw what I can only describe as a caricature of an Asian person looking back at me—one with a terribly swollen face and a swollen body too.

"Mommmm!" I moaned loudly.

She took one look at me and rushed me to her doctor.

Now Doctor Robson was a lady doctor who had served as a missionary for many years in remote areas of the world. Her sharp and inquisitive mind had developed some amazing treatments for a whole assortment of maladies. Before she could use one of those treatments on me, I had to strip to my fruit of the loom's with a lady in the room—not something a modest six year-old boy is about to do without a fight. But, the truth is I was just too miserable to fight. You see, my poison oak was all over my body, but under the skin. So I didn't itch, I just hurt, couldn't see, and was thoroughly miserable.

Dr. Robson had me lay under a special light for two 30-minute sessions that day and, *voila*, the poison oak was gone the next day and I've been immune ever since.

Colby evidently acquired his immunity bit-by-bit by prolonged propinquity. I came to understand this process a little better a few years later when I took a college course in botany. My professor told me that, outside of grass (and she meant the short green stuff, not the stuff the hippies brought into our county a few years later when they left their hearts in San Francisco but brought their pot to southern Oregon)— as I was saying, outside of grass, poison oak is the most populous plant in the county.

Now let's get back to that inaccessible channel in the river. If the poison oak wasn't a sufficient deterrent to approaching the channel from the river bank, then the rest of the vegetation would suffice, because it was such a tangled jungle of bushes, trees, and vines that you would need a machete to hack your way through. And, even if you were able to do that, you still couldn't poke a fishing pole through the willows overhanging the bank to get a hook into the water, let alone to cast your line.

If you wanted to try to get on the island and fish the channel from there, good luck! There was swift, deep water between the far side of the river and the island. You would have to ford the river, getting to the far side, then swim back through swift water to the island. That wasn't feasible. Neither was using a boat because this portion of the river was not navigable—too many very shallow, rocky rapids both above and below the island.

About now you are probably wondering why Colby and I even bothered about the channel with all the obstacles to fishing it. We persisted because Colby had a plan that he hadn't revealed to me yet and because he was as determined as the plan was shrewd.

When we reached the river, we parked our bicycles—we hadn't graduated to motorcycles yet—and headed downstream to a very shallow rapids where we forded the river carrying our fishing gear. Once on the other side, we walked back upstream, even with the upper part of the island. That's when Colby clued me in on how we were going to get onto that island.

You see Colby had learned that where the current splits to flow around the island, there is a very narrow ridge on the river bottom were a lot of gravel and sand were deposited by the peculiar flow pattern of the river.

"I don't know how deep it gets as you walk the little ridge, or even if it goes all the way across to the island," Colby informed me.

"Let's give it a try," I responded.

You see those unknowns didn't bother me because, worst case, we'd just get swept away. I had already been swept off my feet and taken down stream, wallet, fishing gear, and all, about five miles upstream (below Grayback Park). The worst thing that could happen if you got swept away was that the ink on your fishing license might bleed until was unreadable. If it was unreadable and you fished anyway, and a game warden came, you were at the mercy of his good will.

I plunged in after Colby and tried to tight rope walk that narrow little under-water ridge without letting the current knock me off from it. If that happened, you were immediately in much swifter, deeper water and it was "*bon boyage*" because you were going to go about 200 yards downstream where you would be deposited in a 10 foot deep hole—our hot summer day swimming hole, Roger's hole.

As Colby and I crossed, the water topped out about thigh high just before we reached the island. We kept our balance, our footing, our fishing gear, and now we were on the island. We quickly crossed the island pushing aside the bushes in our way, and excitedly began examining the channel from our new vantage point.

What we saw in no way diminished our enthusiasm. The current was moderate and steady. The water was fairly deep and thick willows overhung the river bank creating a cool, shady haven for big-lunker trout even on a hot summer day.

Now anybody can catch those stupid little four- or five-inch trout. They bite anything that moves, anytime of the day. They'll strike a bare hook without any bait as well as a spinner that's twice their size. Their eyes are bigger than their mouths or stomachs.

Colby and I weren't going for small trout, not even legal six to eight inch fish. We were looking for the place where the big guys hang out. We knew that this river had a lot of big rainbows in it. Colby and I knew they had to be somewhere and also that they had to eat some time. Under that shady bank along the channel was the most likely place we had ever seen on this fork of the Illinois River. It looked right—even smelled right. The place just reeked of big trout!

We rigged up, both with eggs (I had won Colby over) and since the island was about 100 yards long, we spread a safe casting distance apart and started casting for the opposite bank. We were trying to place our bait under the overhanging willows where our eggs could sink down and drift through several feet of prime big-lunker habitat before we had to reel in and cast again. Getting just the right touch on our casts proved challenging. Each of our first two casts got hung up in the willows, resulting in us breaking our lines and having to rig up again—I hate rigging up, especially when you should actually be fishing.

Finally persistence paid off and both Colby and I got off a long series of near-perfect casts into that perfect water that filled the next two perfect hours with perfect fishing. After a couple of good casts each, we both pulled in 15-inch rainbows.

That was when I asked, "Colby, did you bring the fish stringer?"

"No, I thought you had it."

Neither of us had brought the stringer and we had two 15-inch trout to do something with. So Colby put down his pole and cut a big piece of willow with a fork on one end. We had already put our two big fish out of their misery and so we slipped them onto the makeshift stringer.

Well, to make a long story short, Colby and I meticulously swept the entire length of the channel and found ourselves at the lower tip of the island with a stringer full of 12- to 18-inch rainbows. We had both nearly limited out. We were ecstatic and couldn't wait to get home and tell Colby's folks, our friends, and I couldn't wait to tell my Grandpa.

I led the way to the upper end of the island and, since I now knew the way, I began tight rope walking the underwater ridge line across to the far bank of the river. Colby, with the willow branch firmly tucked in his belt, followed me through the strong current that accelerated as the island split it.

As I stepped onto the river bank I yelled back at Colby, "Please hold up that stringer for me one more time, it's a beautiful sight!"

Colby had just emerged from the deep, swift part of the river, so he pulled the branch on his belt free and held it up in all of its glory—the branch that no longer had a fork at the bottom to hold the fish—the branch from which just slid the last big rainbow I caught—the branch that was now just sickeningly empty.

Willows are green, easy to cut, easy to bend, but are often easily split because of their greenness. The forked part of our stringer had been stripped off by the weight of the fish and the pull of the thigh-high current. Likewise, we had been stripped— stripped of the evidence of our fishing heroics.

Of course we told everyone about the stringer full of big trout we caught on that unlikely day. But everyone, to a person, even my Grandpa, just winked and nodded, laughing at our tall tail of the ones that got away even after they were dead.

As we were telling our story, somewhere down toward the mouth of the Rogue River (of which the Illinois River is a major tributary) a seagull, or perhaps a bald eagle, is feasting on one of the ones that got away. May they choke on it!

Now that isn't the end of the story. My Grandpa was about to get a little taste of his own winking and nodding medicine. You see my Grandpa and the whole clan (down to the first cousins anyway) spent several days together near Brookings, Oregon camping at a beach park. The guys did a lot of fishing off the huge rock that extended about 200 yards into the ocean.

Colby came along to keep me company. Very quickly Colby, Grandpa, and I became fishing buddies. The three of us got up really early one morning, long before the others and even before breakfast. We grabbed our poles, our shrimp bait, and headed for the end of that big rock where we could cast down into a 50-foot deep hole. Perched on rock seats about five feet above the lazy swells that flowed by, we started catching sea perch that ranged from one to three pounds. That was perfect for me, as I was using my light weight reel, 10-pound test line and 2-pound test leader.

I let one cast really fly into the deepest water I could reach. Shortly after casting I pulled on my line a little and got that sickening feedback that tells you you're hung up on seaweed on the bottom. When in that fix you have two choices—first, pull hard to break your leader, reel in and rig up again or second, wait until a few swells pass and hope they disentangle your line allowing you to keep fishing.

Well, I've already said that I hate rigging up my line when I should be fishing, so I decided to wait it out. While I hate rigging up, I do know the importance of doing it right. When we fish in the ocean, we usually use a 4- to 6-ounce lead weights. Now, using a lighter leader than your line and attaching the weight properly can spare you problems and sometimes pain. I saw one fellow rig up without leader. When he got hung up he just pulled harder and harder until his big pole bent double. That's when his line broke, but left his weight attached. He bounced a 6-ounce weight off his forehead, which left a giant goose egg.

When you are hung up in seaweed, your line usually gives a gentle pull with the passage of each swell. As I felt these little tugs that day they seemed to be saying to me, "Feel that? That's all you're gonna' feel until you break your leader, reel in and start all over again." As I felt one such mocking little tug, it was accompanied by a pulsating tug that lasted a bit longer.

I hollered over to Grandpa and Colby, "My pole just jerked a couple times. It wasn't the seaweed!"

They knew I'd been hung up for a while, but Grandpa suggested, "Wait a couple minutes before you give up and break your line. Maybe there's a big one sniffing around your bait." Grandpa had no more than spoken those words when my line really started pulling, broke free from the seaweed and was meandering all around the deep hole. I was totally unprepared for this turn of events—had not even set my drag on, I was in free-wheeling mode—a cardinal sin for an experienced fisherman. As a result I was plunged into a real battle with the fish and a battle with my reel. All I could do was reel forward and backward as fast as I could to keep up with the fish, which was obviously much bigger than my two-pound test leader tied to my ten-pound test line.

Colby and Grandpa stopped fishing to watch the show. All eyes were on me. There I was with my little trout pole bent double at times reeling in and out, looking like a moron but desperately trying to prevent the monster that had my hook in its mouth from breaking my line. Fool or not, I was not about to just let this big guy get away without putting everything I had into landing him.

Well what ever was on my line decided to head out to sea, so I started reeling backward with super speed until most of my line was out. Then the big fish turned toward me and I reeled in with super speed. Now, I've got pretty fast reflexes, but after 20 minutes of repeats of the fish's maneuvers, it felt like my wrists were turning to rubber. Just as I was about to give up and quit this game of tug of war, I felt the fish's tug grow much weaker—he was tiring. Now that I didn't have to continuously maintain tension by hand, I quickly reached over with my left hand flipped on the drag and twisted my drag by an amount I hoped would be close—it was close enough. So slowly I worked the big fish close to the rock.

The first time he came to the surface I yelled, "He's all head!"

You see his mouth was about a foot in diameter, and then his body tapered quickly to a tiny tail. He was about 3 feet long, probably over 30 pounds, 20 pounds of which was head. My little number six hook stuck in one corner of the giant mouth reminded me of David and his slingshot standing before Goliath. I thought I could hear the Goliath of the fish say, "What am I, a dog, that you should stick a number six hook in my lip and try to land me on two-pound test leader?"

I didn't care what the fish thought about me as long as I actually could land him. Grandpa was trying his best to help me do just that. It was almost impossible to climb down to water level on the big rock because there were no hand or foot holds close to the water and you had to watch out for the swells. But Grandpa did it!

As I carefully pulled the big cod to the edge of the rock, carefully keeping time with the swells, Grandpa was having his own battle with the fish. It looked like Grandpa was playing chicken with the cod and its huge tooth-filled the mouth. Every time Grandpa reached to grab the fish by the gills, the fish's head would swivel around and snap at Grandpa's fingers.

Why did we have to forget the gaff hook this morning? This is what gaff hooks are made for.

Out of frustration and the fisherman's drive to never let one get away, Grandpa bit the bullet and decided to let the big fish bite him. He had just started to shove his hand down the fish's mouth to grab the gills from inside, a virtual death grip, when the currently passing swell moved by, and the big fish fell with the passage of the swell and my line fell slack against the rock.

After 30 minutes, friction with the cod's mouth had worn my leader in two. The cod just lay there for 30 seconds or so then, realizing he was free, turned and swam along the surface to the middle of the deep hole—probably just to prolong my agony—then dove deep.

As the fish sank to the bottom our hearts sank with the realization that, though we had that cod against the rock for 10 minutes or more, he was gone and there would be no hero's welcome back in camp for the conquering fisherman. There would be no pictures of me with the big cod and no cod fillets for dinner that night.

To his credit Grandpa gave it his best shot. He told the story with great gusto as only Grandpa could tell it, but no one was buying the truth about the big one that got away.

For Colby and me, many more positive fishing adventures lie ahead, like the time Colby's Dad called home from work just to tell us that Fish and Game had just released thousands of eight- to ten-inch rainbows into the Illinois River just below our favorite stretch of water. We grabbed our gear and peddled hard for the fishing hole. We started fishing our way down the river toward the release point. Every time we dropped our baited hooks into a likely spot, we pulled out a nice trout. Soon we had both limited, so we pedaled home, cleaned our fish, stuck them in the freezer, and headed back for the river. We repeated that cycle three times that day putting sixty nice, pan-sized trout in the freezer (minus the ones we ate for dinner that night).

Yes, when you fish enough, after awhile it all seems to come out in the wash. It mostly averages out over a long period of time—all except for those times you tell the truth and still no one believes you about the ones that got away.

32
Beach Logs Can Kill

Now that I've become an old geezer that lives in Washington State, I love the coast, especially that portion that is in the Olympic National Park. There's one beautiful, rugged beach called Rialto Beach that my wife, Babe, and I love to hike. Just as you approach the beach there's a big sign put up by the park rangers—actually all the beaches on the Olympic Peninsula have it. The sign tells you the truth when it says, "Beach logs can kill!"

It was a day in early August that Colby's sister, A.J., wanted to go see a friend in northern California over on the coast. I was staying a few days at Colby's, so when those words "the coast" were uttered, the speaker had our utter attention.

Colby then approached his Mom with a couple of questions. First, could Colby and I ride along? Second, could we stop near Crescent City and get in some beach time?

Colby's Mom said yes to both of our requests, so we grabbed an extra pair of cut-off jeans, hopped into the car and waited impatiently for our first glimpse of the ocean. Two hours later, when we got it, it was beautiful! No clouds, warm, even on the beach, and after dropping off A.J. we found a nice beach with lots of sand as well as some rocks and driftwood to explore.

Colby and I hadn't been in the water more than a few minutes when we spotted something swimming just outside the breaking waves. It was big! Just as I was about to start moving closer to safety of the beach, I saw the thing get lifted up by a large swell—it didn't have a dorsal fin.

"Colby," I hollered, "It's a big log! Let's go get it!"

Since the log was now only about 30 yards beyond where we were bobbing in the waves, Colby yelled back, "Race you to it!"

We really didn't need to race to it because that big swell pushed the log almost to where we were standing, chest deep in icy west-coast ocean water. On a 90-degree day, icy is good, but the beach log was bad—we just needed to find that out for ourselves. There were no signs to tell you such things in 1959.

Well, Colby swam out along one side of the log and I took the other side. By swimming it and by placing our feet on the bottom and gently pushing it, we nudged that languid log into water that was about four feet deep.

"It looks like a chunk of a big fir tree or maybe a redwood," Colby commented after inspecting the titanic chunk of timber.

"What ever it is, it sure is waterlogged. It barely floats above water."

"That's O.K., makes it easier to grab hold of," Colby commented—an assertion he was about to revoke.

"We'd better keep this big beast pointed straight toward the shore. If it gets turned sideways, the least bit of a wave will take it right out of our hands."

"Yeah, and we should both stay on the sides of it or the least bit of a wave will push this waterlogged battering ram right into us," Colby wisely suggested.

About that time Colby's Mom hollered from the sandy beach where she was reading, "You boys be careful with that log!"

Most times when Moms do that you can just ignore'm because you already know what they're warning you about. In our ignorance that's exactly what we did—we ignored her.

Right about then Colby was on one side, I was on the other, and the log, which probably weighed well over a ton, was pointed perpendicular to the shore and thus to the waves. A fairly large but gentle wave lifted the log up. I stepped a little closer to steady our floating friend. But a funny thing happened when the wave passed. Have you ever noticed how the bigger a wave is, the bigger the dip in the water before and after it is?

Well the remnants of a previous wave were running back out to sea, so when the incoming wave crossed the out-going wave something happened that I did not understand at the time. Many years later, in my meteorological coursework, we studied wave motion extensively because we used waves to model and to predict atmospheric flow. We studied long waves, short, faster moving waves, and in the tropics and subtropics, easterly waves. We studied waves losing amplitude and increasing their amplitude and the physical factors that produce those effects. How I wish I was wave-aware in 1959.

What had happened when the two waves crossed and when I stepped closer to our log, is that the amplitude of the two combined waves raised the log higher than either wave alone could have done. When the crest of the two waves left, the bottom of the two waves combined dropping the log much more than either wave, by itself, would have dropped it.

Even with the big drop of the log, I probably would've been okay if the log had been completely round. But it was not round on its underside; it bulged out on the part of the underside that was over my foot—the underside that got dropped on to the top of my right foot.

I hollered, "Aaahhh!" or something like that, when the log crunched straight down on the top part of my foot; but, when the next wave slid the log along the top of my foot, I really screamed.

The scream caught Colby's Mom's attention, as did all the blood on my foot that she saw as I hobble hopped up the beach to her, the nearest thing to medical help for miles around. She found some kind of medicine in the car, but had to grab the cleanest piece of cloth we could find to wrap the rapidly swelling and still bleeding foot in. Then we made a beeline for the nearest drugstore which was in Crescent City, where we got gauze and some antibiotic cream to dress my wound—some stuff the druggist recommended.

Now let me tell you my foot really smarted and the initial wound with all the skin scraped off the top of my foot and all of the blood made for an ugly sight. But that wasn't nearly as bad as what happened to me four years earlier.

My folks and Colby's folks had stopped to get water from the coolest, most refreshing-est spring in the world, after a trip to the beach. You had to go about 50 yards down the hill from the parking area to get to the water. I jumped out of the car and sprinted straight down the hillside, ignoring the winding walking trail. Just about the time I hit full speed down the hill, something hooked me by one eye. It hooked me so hard that my feet swung up in front of me. The hook then let go dropping me from about 6 feet up in the air right onto my back.

I screamed as blood poured from my eye. My Mom completely freaked out when she saw me. My eye was so full of blood that we all assumed it was just a hole in my face with no eyeball left in it. That thought made me holler even louder.

It turned out that someone had hung a piece of barbwire from a tree limb and turned it up like a hook on the bottom. It had hooked me just under my eyelid and swung my whole body up into the air as I was running about 20 miles per hour down the hill. Fortunately, it just lacerated the underside of my eyelid and ripped some of the muscles that work my eyelid. That all healed up with no permanent damage.

Well now that my foot didn't hurt quite as bad, I began worrying about permanent damage, especially since football practice was supposed to start in one week.

When we got back to Colby's house, his Mom called my Mom, my parents picked me up late that afternoon and the next morning our doctor was using his newly installed X-ray machine on my foot. When Dr. Johnson asked me how this happened, I said, "You know, beach logs are dangerous." He got the picture immediately. Almost as immediately he got the pictures of my foot from his brand new machine.

The good news was, my foot had no broken bones, just something called an obtrusive abrasion. That means the log had bruised a bunch of bones down deep inside my foot and then scraped all the skin, and what little meat's on the top of my foot, clear off. The bad news was that, though I was young, healthy and would heal quickly, I would miss at least the first two weeks of football practice. This was mostly because my foot was so swollen I couldn't get my football shoe on my right foot (we had to wear high tops in those days because the coaches were worried about ankle injuries). There was no way that foot could turn a corner and slide down into the part of the shoe where it belonged, until the swelling went considerably down.

For two weeks we iced it, soaked it in Epsom salts, and did every other thing the doctor suggested until at last, three weeks later, my foot slipped down into the shoe. The next day I was dying in 95-degree weather in two-a-day practices while wondering if I should re-injure my foot and let it heal until the weather cooled off a bit.

Let me conclude this story by saying that NEVER again did Colby and I ever play with logs in the surf. Also, each time you go to the coast and see one of those warning signs, you'd better believe them—beach logs can kill—or hurt you so bad you wish they had.

33
Buckin' Hay And Buckin' Bales

It was the hardest work a boy could find. It was just about the only work a boy could find. We tried to make it fun and we did until Colby tried to ride buckin' bales while buckin' hay.

The summer after my junior year, Colby and I both needed to earn a little money. I wanted to buy some of my own school clothes and I really needed to bore out the engine of my Honda to get a little more horsepower. Colby had plans too. But, what we didn't have, and what was so hard to come by in those days, was a summer job.

The logging and lumber industries were booming in Oregon, but there were no temporary jobs there. This was before most of the fast-food establishments even existed, so you couldn't just go flip hamburgers under the golden arches. Even the girls had to compete for the few waitress jobs at the A&W.

There was one job only the guys could do—too physically demanding for the girls—but even that job, buckin' hay, was hard to find. So when Colby and I heard that the senior Mr.

Powell, who provided the hay for his son's dairy, needed a couple of boys to bring in two barns full of hay, we were over there at his farm on Holland Loop Road in a flash. Little did we know how much hay two barns can hold and how much work is involved in getting that much hay from the fields to nice stacks in the barn. But we were about to learn.

You see, buckin' hay is like this. You pile the bales of hay from the field one at a time on a truck, stacking bales up to as high as 10 feet—what ever the truck can hold without dumping the load. Have you ever lifted a 120-pound bale 10 feet into the air? Once the truck is loaded, it's driven to the barn where you once again handle each bale of hay. Now handling a bale of hay means picking it up, lifting it onto the truck, then pulling it off and stacking it. The bales weighed anywhere from 50 to 120 pounds, depending upon what was growing in the field, and each bale was bound tightly by either wire or twine. Either one would cut into your fingers each time you lifted the bale and you lifted a thousand bales per day. No type of gloves could remove the pain of the wire and twine as they cut into the joints of your fingers.

You continued doing this job in the hot sun (high temperatures ninety-five to one hundred degrees) working from 6:00 AM until 6:00 PM for weeks until the barns were filled. You did all that work for minimum wage, which was, at the time, $1.25 per hour.

At first glance, buckin' hay doesn't sound like very much fun. To Colby and me, it didn't sound like fun after the third or fourth glance, so we decided to work at making it fun.

The first fun thing we found was the old pelican. That was the World War II vintage army truck Mr. Powell bought and converted into a flatbed truck for hauling hay. After observing Colby and me at work for a couple of days, Mr. Powell thought he could trust us, so he just gave us the keys to the old pelican and told us which fields to work on each day. The rest was up to Colby and me and we tried hard to make the rest fun.

When most guys bucked hay, somebody drove and somebody stacked hay on the truck. If you were lucky, there was a third guy who was on the truck to grab the bale and stack it for you. Every so often you switched places. Well for us, it was just Colby and me.

"Hey, Col!" I hollered, "Checkout this granny gear!"

I was going to shift down a gear to get to granny, but when I tried to shove the gear shift ahead, all I got was a grinding noise.

"Doggone it! I forgot these old transmissions aren't synchromesh," I complained.

You had to double clutch to manually synchronize the gears before shifting or you really heard some horrible grinding noise. You also got a great buzz in your hand from the gearshift. I finally got the old pelican into granny gear as we rolled out onto the hay field we were going to work this morning.

"Now watch this," I said to Colby as I opened the driver's door, got out of the truck and let it roll along at one-half a mile per hour as I stood outside.

"You thinking what I'm thinking?" Colby asked, knowing all along what I was thinking and what we both were already envisioning—that is how we could buck hay twice as fast and twice as easy.

"Yep, this job just got a whole lot easier. I'll leave the driver's window down and we can just point the pelican down a row of bales and jerk the wheel through the window if the old bird wonders off line too much," I proclaimed summarizing our idea.

Our job did get a lot easier and we got much faster, doing the job of three boys with just two. This made Mr. Powell happy and we wanted to keep him happy, not only for the job, but also because of the dinner-break thing.

You see, Mr. and Mrs. Powell had come from a farm in the south, and so had their big meal at lunch time. Mrs. Powell served us a huge spread every day, and it was free!

We had roast beef, mashed potatoes and gravy, corn, biscuits and a lot of other food. Then we had desert! We usually had several pies to choose from, *ala mode* of course. To top that off, Mr. Powell told us interesting stories about his growing up years. The stories went on for forty-five minutes on most days. So Colby and I got a super meal and a break from 11:30 AM until 1:30 PM with entertainment thrown in. We weren't gonna do anything to jeopardize that, because two working boys can work up a huge hunger from 6:00 AM to 11:30 AM when they're buckin' hay. You can see why we worked hard and didn't want to rock the boat. Looking back, I think Mr. Powell understood exactly what he was doing by being generous.

Besides the meal and the stories, Mr. Powell was full of a lot of other surprises. I couldn't believe it when Colby and I walked in for lunch one day and Mr. Powell was singing the number one song on the pop charts. I didn't even think old guys like him knew about the charts, let alone actually liked and could sing any of the songs. The song was even one I liked—it was a strange folk song from Australia. They used a saw for the rhythm, creating a weird and wonderful sound.

Now I liked most everything from Australia, the Outback, their unofficial, but *de facto*, national anthem, roo's and wallabies. Well, I liked everything except their stonefish—the box jelly fish was nasty too and that huge saltwater crocodile gave me the creeps—I didn't care for that inland taipan snake with venom about three hundred times as poisonous as our timber rattlers. But I sure liked that song about the old stockman that was dying!

Yes, Mr. Powell constantly surprised Colby and me. One day when we came to work we noticed another person heading our way. He introduced himself and said he would be there to help us for a while. Bit by bit as we worked, he told us a part of his story and we managed to coax the rest out of him.

Orie was about ten years older than Colby and me and had been a trucker. A few months before, his truck had been involved in a fatal traffic accident. It was purely an accident, he wasn't at fault, but the trucking company didn't want the stigma of a driver who had been involved in a fatal accident, so they fired him.

Orie had a wife and a baby, so Mr. Powell offered him a job doing anything Orie could do to help around the farm. He gave Orie's family the vacant ranch hand's house just up the road rent-free for as long as Orie worked for him. And he gave them the noon meal too.

Mr. Powell was a good and generous man—also a good judge of character, which Colby and I could see as we worked with Orie.

One problem with the old pelican that bit Colby and I occasionally was that no matter how well we stacked the load, the old flatbed truck sometimes dumped half of it as we crossed the irrigation canal to exit the fields. Once when that happened I was driving using the low granny gear. But going that slow just exposed the load to the steep angle for a longer period of time. Colby was riding on top of the hay, catching a little breeze to cool off—it was near one hundred degrees that afternoon.

Well, about halfway through crossing the ditch, a hay avalanche started and it buried Colby in 120-pound alfalfa bales. I was surprised when he came up out of hay uninjured.

He learned a valuable lesson about hay avalanches. Don't try to fight them—roll with the hay and keep moving along with the bales and you'll be okay. If you fight it and get stopped, you'll get knocked silly by some alfalfa bale that weighs as much as you do and which hasn't stopped. After the lesson, we had to restack all the hay on the truck.

Well, Orie really helped us with our hay-avalanche problem. He brought along a couple of long ropes one day and after we had loaded up the old pelican Orie asked, "Would you guys like me to show you the trucker's knot?"

Colby said, "Sure, we'd like to see it." Orie could tell we were clueless, so he explained it as he was using it to tie down the bales on the old pelican.

"You see the trucker's knot gives you a way to cinch up a rope almost like you had a block and tackle rigged up. When we get these ropes over those bales, not a single bale will budge when we the cross that irrigation canal," Orie explained as he quickly and deftly flipped ropes over the load and then cinched them down really tight.

"Let's try another rope just for good measure. Come here Colby, you tie this one."

In no time he had Colby tying that knot, and then he had me use the rest of the rope to tie the knot on the other side of the load. Colby and I both learned that knot and we sure put it to good use.

After a couple of weeks Colby and I lost Orie to a trucking company that was willing to take a chance on him. But we never lost another bale of hay off the old pelican—not as long as we used Orie's trucker's knot.

As an old geezer, I still use a variation of the knot Orie taught us nearly a half century ago. The state of Washington passed a law invoking heavy fines if you don't secure the load you're hauling. Each time I cinch down the tarp over a load of junk headed for the dump my wife, Babe, says, "Stop wasting time with that silly rope—let's get going."

I just smile to myself and finish tying Orie's knot. I've never lost a twig even on the biggest load that my little truck has hauled.

Thank you, Orie for helping Colby and me when we desperately needed to keep our loads on the old pelican. And thank you, Mr. Powell, for giving Orie a job when he desperately needed one.

As that summer wore on, Colby and I went from experiencing buckin' hay to experiencing buckin' bales. You see, we were filling a second barn and this barn had a door in the top above the main barn door to put the hay through so we could fill the barn to the brim with hay. When the hay got so high in the barn that we needed to use the upper door, Mr. Powell brought out his hay bale elevator.

That contraption had a chute that we could extended from the ground up to and through the top barn door. The chute had a belt that traveled up the chute on the topside and down it on the bottom side. On the topside, the belt had little crosspieces to catch a bale of hay, take it up the chute, and launch it out into space at the top. The elevator was powered by the drive on the rear of Mr. Powell's tractor

After Mr. Powell showed us how to set up, connect to the tractor and use the elevator, he left and we went to work on the load we had just brought over on the old pelican. I started at the bottom pitching the bales into the chute. Colby grabbed and stacked them after they were launched through the barn door by the elevator.

After a bit I got tired and the sun was very hot that day. So Colby, who had been working in the shade of the barn, agreed to trade places. Well I was really tired—too tired almost to climb up into the top of the barn. So I tossed a big bale of alfalfa onto the elevator and leaped onto its back like Captain Ahab on Moby Dick. I road that whale of a bale to the top and then leaped off to the side landing in the hay as the big whale of a bale breached coming off the elevator and then bounced on the rising hay floor in the barn beside me.

"Colby, that worked pretty slick. You oughta' try it when we trade places again," I suggested.

Well, Colby tried it all right. Most guys want to get in their eight seconds on the bronco after they get out of the chute. Colby got more than eight seconds in the chute, but when he came out of the chute, well that buckin' bronc of a bale bucked Colby off. When the bale tipped over the edge at the top of the chute, it sort of just tipped upside down and Colby was still hanging on. When Colby realized the trick this moo food mustang had played on him, he finally let go. Unfortunately this left the bale right above him and unfortunately he had also chosen a big, 120-pound alfalfa bale.

As it turned out, Colby got crunched really good by that bale. I think it knock the wind out of him. He didn't complain, but neither did he play anymore, or resume work, for about ten minutes—that's just about how long it took me to recover when I really got the wind knocked out of me in football.

Using all the tricks we had learned that summer, in less than a week more, Colby and I filled the barn to the very peak. Mr. Powell declared that the work was done and he paid us plenty enough for me to get my school clothes (the ones I, not my Mom, picked out) and to have my Honda engine bored out. Colby and I finished that summer with a lot more muscle than we'd ever had before, some cash, sore fingers, and in Colby's case, sore ribs that he got from buckin' hay and buckin' bales.

34
From Daisies To Remingtons

If you were male and lived in southern Oregon in the '50s, guns were a part of your life. Colby got his first BB gun at five. I got mine at six. While I didn't like having to be a year older to get my first real shooting gun, I could live with that. What I could not live with was Colby getting his first 22 rifle at age seven and I had to wait until I was ten to get mine.

If you're horrified at the thought of two ten year-olds roaming the countryside with 22 rifles, there are some things that you need to understand. Colby and I were raised around guns just like some of you were raised around city streets, where cars whiz by at speeds well above the speed limit. You were taught to watch out for traffic, but by the age at which you learned to stay safe around traffic, we were already several years into our gun education.

Some of my earliest memories of guns were when I was three or four, seeing my Grandpa sitting in his chair cleaning his guns. He would call me over and explain that even if a gun is empty, or even incapable of firing, you never point it at anything you don't intend to shoot.

Grandpa and my Dad took me to target practice and I saw how carefully they handled their guns. Finally the day came when they let me fire one of their hunting rifles at a target. Of course I felt a little more grown-up, and of course I wanted to hit the bull's-eye, but even more than these, I felt a deep sense of responsibility.

Colby's Dad taught him the same stuff about guns that I was taught.

At nine or ten years old, with six or seven years of gun education, I was still playing cowboys with my toy guns. That would really ruffle some feathers today. I can just hear it on the 5 o'clock news, "In the morning kids play with cap guns and in the afternoon they roam the hills with 22s!"

To Colby and me, the difference between toy guns and real guns was most certainly not a matter of degree; it was a matter of category. The distinction between the two was so clear that we didn't have to even think about it.

When we played cowboys, the words "play like" preceded every scene of our western dramas.

"Play like you're the sheriff and I'm the outlaw and you come to arrest me."

"Play like I'm Roy and you're Gabby."

"No I had to be Gabby last time!"

"Okay, play like I'm Roy and your Dale Evans."

"No way!"

However, the words "play like" never entered our conversations when real guns were in our hands.

My first BB gun was a long-barreled Daisy. A lot of kids wanted Red Ryder BB guns like in that movie, <u>The Christmas Story</u>. Well, my Daisy had a longer barrel and more compression so it shot harder and straighter than a Red Ryder. How I loved that Daisy.

Now I don't want you to think that I thought I was perfect, or that I even came close to being a little angel—I did not. Like most boys who lived in the country, I felt the juvenile flavor of "me great hunter," and so I tried to prove that I was.

The first things I went after were birds. Yeah, I know—you don't have to tell me how you feel about that. But as of yet, I had no negative feelings when snuffing out the life from a sparrow, a wren, or even a robin. I bagged my first bird at age seven—shot him out of an oak tree near my Grandmother's house. I was now officially a hunter! I thought birds and BBs were meant to be together, like real hard together. Colby was like-minded.

For three or four years I shot birds without remorse. I thought about notching the wooden stock in my Daisy but, hey, I needed to have enough wood left to put against my shoulder.

I can still remember clearly the day it happened. Things like that get indelibly etched into our memories. The bytes are burned into our ROM and there they remain until our computer lets out all of its smoke (you may have observed that computers without their smoke can't run anymore).

My day came when I was standing alone by the fence in the field on the west side of our property. The little wren just flew up and lit only seven or eight feet from me. I thought to myself, "He's dead!" I raised my BB gun while staring into the bird's eye, pulled the trigger, and he was.

Immediately there was a deep ache somewhere inside of me. I hadn't felt anything like that since when I was five years old my little cocker spaniel, Skeeter, tried to cross the highway to meet me and was hit by a car in front of my eyes. He continued running up into my arms where he died in a few short seconds. When I shot the wren, that was the type of pain I felt—maybe not of the same degree, but of the same category. It was a deep sense of loss—a loss that should have been, and could have been, avoided.

I tried to wrestle with my feelings. What had I lost? All I could come up with was that a little bird, full of life had just died. Why had it happened? The answer, at my whim. Why did I "whim" it to be? For that I had no answer.

This was one tiny step in the process of God drawing a young boy's heart to himself. He had softened a once calloused part of my conscience by pushing a splinter into the quick—it sure hurt. I was sorry for taking the bird's life. I was sorry for all the birds' lives that I had ever taken. I was just plain sorry.

As best I can remember, I never intentionally shot another bird except for the few game birds I later killed for food—except for that "accident" when Colby and I were plinking on the rattlesnake hill.

Colby and I headed out across the field that we had burned while playing firebug. We also crossed the second field were my 300-yard arrow shot had gone and began walking up the long hill that was mostly a big hillside meadow, leading toward the rattlesnake hill. At the far end of the meadow was a tall ponderosa pine of the 120-foot tall variety. In the top of the tree, about 400 yards away, I could see the silhouette of a bird on the very top of the tree—just a black dot against the sky.

I looked over at Colby and said, "Watch this."

"You really think you can hit that? Your gun can hardly shoot that far," Colby said not taunting me as much as implying, "Why waste a bullet on an impossible shot?"

I gave him a squinty-eyed look and started going through the motions that Clint Eastwood used in the final scene of <u>The Good The Bad And The Ugly</u>. But these were my own moves because Clint was still Rowdy Yates at the time.

After all my coolness had been used up and I had sighted in on the bird with my open sight, allowing for the little 22 slug to drop several feet in the intervening 400 yards, I squeezed the trigger. The report of the rifle was followed immediately by the bird dropping 120 feet to the ground.

I was stunned. Colby was silent. I hadn't intended to kill anything. What had I killed? I didn't even know, so I began trotting toward the fallen bird.

I arrived at the big pine tree and became heartsick. There at my feet lay a beautiful meadowlark with a bullet hole perfectly placed in the notch of the black V on the bird's breast. This is the stuff gunfighter legends were made of in the old west, but I didn't want this to be any part of my legacy. I was only reminded of the wren and the BB gun, and of course, the $500 fine for shooting the Oregon state bird, which I had just done.

A meadowlark's song is so cheery and full of life that I had begun imitating it as a little boy. Mom laughed at my crude attempts to sound like a meadowlark. She would not be laughing now. Neither was I.

Right then, I modified Grandpa's old adage, "Don't point a gun at anything you don't intend to shoot," to a more appropriate saying that I now intended to follow, "Never point a gun at anything you don't want to be dead."

About an hour after the meadowlark incident, Colby and I walked to the top of the rattlesnake hill. There I was nearly bitten by a rattler. This was one of those incidents where, upon reflection, you can see what can only be understood as God's protection. For no reason that I could think of at the time, I felt that I should not walk by the bush just ahead beside the trail. I had a very strong sense that I just should not do that.

I hollered at Colby, who had taken another route to the top of the hill, "Hey Col! Wait up!"

As I studied the bush beside the trail, I saw something slowly oscillating back and forth under it. I moved to get a better viewing angle and saw a good-sized rattler coiled in the striking position and doing that little head dance they sometimes do before striking. In a couple of seconds more, I would have given him an easy shot at my ankle. This rattler uncharacteristically gave no warning rattle; he just waited to strike.

I called Colby over and pointed out the sneaky snake. Then I shot sneaky snake's head off—completely off. Standing there mesmerized, Colby and I timed the strikes of the headless snake. For thirty minutes the rattler coiled and struck until his brain, that is partially distributed along the snake's spine, ran out of life sustaining nutrients and the electrochemical energy was all expended. Then the headless snake behaved as I believed all rattlers should—it lay dead, with no means of biting anyone or anything anymore.

Though Colby and I were gun-educated and didn't think we ever endangered other people's lives while hunting or plinking, we sometimes did things that we really shouldn't have done. One time that comes to mind was when Colby had his own "meadowlark" experience.

Colby and I, with our 22s were heading up toward the road leading to the limestone caves. We seldom took our guns when going up to the caves, there were too many fun things to do up there that didn't, or couldn't, involve guns. Colby was carrying his lever action 22. He liked the speed in getting off shots that this gun gave him, but he had beaten on the sight with every hammer in his Dad's shop trying to get that gun to shoot straight. Part of its problem was its relatively short barrel and the other part was the messed up sight. You just never knew if you were going to hit what you shot at with that thing. Sometimes it was as accurate as my long-barreled single shot, and other times I could throw a rock straighter than that gun would shoot.

Well we were just approaching the first waterhole along the caves road, so Colby suggested we approached quietly and see if anything was watering. As we slipped in close to the water hole, we heard nothing, so we just gave up and walked right in. That's when we heard the telltale crashing of a fleeing deer.

"Hold it," Colby whispered my direction. "Look up the hill."

Not 30 yards, directly up the steep hill above the water hole, stood a big doe broadside to us and being really still, trying to blend in with the surrounding brush.

"Watch this," Colby whispered.

Where had I heard those words before? "I hope he isn't gonna do something stupid," I thought to myself.

"See the very tip of the doe's tail sticking out behind that bush? I'm just gonna nick it in the tail and send it running," Colby added, sounding super cool.

Oh Colby went through all of that too-cool-to-be-true stuff like Clint Eastwood would do in six years or so. He coolly propped his foot up on a dead bush, coolly rested his elbow on his knee to support his aim, and coolly sighted in on that doe's tail for a good 30 seconds. Next I heard three noises in rapid succession. First, there was a crack as the dead bush supporting Colby's foot broke, thus breaking his whole aim. Second, there was the crack of his gun going off as the breaking bush jerked his whole body, including his trigger finger. Third, there was a crash as the doe dropped straight down—dead!

Then came a fourth noise—a rhythmical thumping with each rotation of the doe's body as it rolled slowly down the hill all the way to our feet. What a powerful way to drive home the message of what our carelessness had just done. I don't think that was coincidence.

I knew Colby was sorry for shooting the doe by accident when that bush broke as he was pulling the trigger. I also knew it was almost impossible to bring down a deer with one shot from a 22, let alone kill it dead with a single shot—especially when your gun was loaded with 22 shorts. But Colby's errant shot had hit the doe high in the neck, severing its spinal cord near the base of the brain and killing it instantly.

When reality finally sank in, we both said in precise unison, "Let's get out of here!"

There was no "Jinx you owe me a Coke" in reply to the replicated phrase, only a realization that we had killed a doe without reason, out of season, and without a doe tag. A beautiful doe was dead and the fine would be about the same as for me killing the meadowlark,— about $500.

I spoke up, "First, we'd better hide it fast and then get out of here. "

"Where can hide it so no one coming by on the road can see it?"

"Let's drag it to the dry wash over to our right and cover it with dead brush," I responded with great urgency in my voice.

That was followed by the realization that I was behaving just like the murderers we saw on the Perry Mason show, and I knew they always got caught and ended up having to confess. Why did I have to think about that just now? After seeing that doe roll down to our feet, we would crumble like a graham cracker if we ran into a Perry Mason-type game warden any time soon.

Well, we had that doe drug and buried in about three minutes flat and then we ran toward home. We told no one what happened and didn't venture up that way for four weeks. When we walked up to the water hole a month later, we took no guns and we made sure no one else was in that part of the woods before going near the spot where we had hidden the unfortunate doe. What we found was only a few bones left behind by the sundry scavengers.

That night we "'fessed up" to Colby's parents about accidentally killing the doe.

"And you just left it up there?" Colby's Mom asked incredulously.

"It was dead, you couldn't undo that, so you shouldn't have let the deer go to waste," Colby's Dad chided.

Well, maybe feeding the bugs, buzzards, and coyotes, could be considered going to waste. But I bet they were happy to get all that meat just handed to them. Regardless, as best I can remember, I never again saw Colby shooting at things he didn't intend to kill after he accidentally killed that doe. But that's not to say Colby never again shot when he shouldn't have.

I think I told you how badly Colby and I hated diggers. For a while we conducted a campaign to eradicate those revolting rodents from our forest. Well, Colby chased one into a big fallen ponderosa pine. The digger ran between the loosening plates of bark and the tree trunk. Noticing where the digger was hiding,

Colby stuck the barrel of this 22 between a hunk of bark and the trunk and he pried off the bark. I should say, "He tried to pry off the bark." However, his gun barrel just bent about 20 degrees to one side.

Nonplussed, Colby took a closer look at the barrel and immediately wondered if his gun was ruined forever or not. The first test he thought of was to fire it. So he did.

Now I felt downright sorry for the little bullet because at 700 miles per hour, it pulled an incredible number of G's as it rounded the corner inside the barrel. I guess that the tremendous friction caused by the tremendous centrifugal force is what caused the gun to sound like it did when Colby shot it, "Bo-eeng!" was the hollow, ricocheting noise we heard. That probably tore the side right off from the unfortunate little bullet as it rubbed against all of those riflings inside of the barrel while rounding that 20-degree corner at Mach 0.9. And who knows where the bullet went—a gun barrel bent 20 degrees sure ain't gonna shoot straight.

Colby really liked that little 22, so he took it back to his Dad's workshop and worked at straightening the barrel with a sledgehammer, using the same big anvil he used when he was presiding as Judge Colby (you can read about his kangaroo court in another story). The gun shot again, but never straight. Furthermore, we never did eradicate all those doggoned digger squirrels. They are still pests that ruin gardens and we still have to put up with their shrill, early-warning alarm every time we enter their domain—"eeenchut, eeenchut!" I hate that sound!

As the number of deer hunters grew in our woods, Colby and I began reading about hunters getting shot, or shot at, even though they were wearing those fluorescent red and yellow colors. We had heard many other hunters' shots while we were deer hunting, but we reasoned that if someone were actually shooting at you, the shot would surely sound a lot different than shots directed elsewhere.

We wanted, no we needed, to be able to recognize the sound of a shot when the muzzle was pointed at us, as well as the sound of a bullet whizzing close by. Since we didn't want to learn the sound accidentally out in the woods, we set up a little experiment, all in the name of safety, where we would shoot at each other with our 30-30 deer rifles. But, don't be alarmed, we did this in a perfectly safe way.

I picked out a three-foot thick black oak for protection (*quercus kelloggii*, sure to stop even a 30-30 bullet). We established the shooting point about 50 yards from the big oak. Then we established the protocol to which we would be bound on our sacred honor (and our lives). The listener would get completely behind the oak tree, but would place one ear near the right side of the tree, still sheltered from any incoming shots. When ready, the listener would yell out, "Ready!" At which time the shooter would raise his rifle, and aim about three feet out from the right side of the oak tree; then he would say, "One, two, three," and then pull the trigger. After the shot he would yell, "Shooter standing down!" At that point, the test would be over. The listener could come out, emerging from the left side of the tree. Then we exchanged places so the shooter could become the listener and hear what was like to be shot at—in a safe manner.

Maybe this was a hare-brained scheme. But, I can tell you this for sure; you can tell when somebody is shooting at you. It sounds completely different from a shot not directed at you. The sound of the shot comes louder and more violently to your ears and there is a nerve-rattling noise that's hard to describe one microsecond after a 30-30 hollow-point bullet passes you at Mach 2.0.

After the experiment, Colby said thankfully, "Man, I'm glad we did that. Now if some drunken hunter up from California, the kind who shoots at anything that moves, shoots at me, I'll know it and can take cover."

"But we still have to rely on him being too drunk to shoot straight or the whole thing is moot," I added, not feeling so sure we were now actually any safer in the woods during deer hunting season.

The reason for my feeling of angst was that when people who haven't been educated about guns get their hands on a rifle, nobody is safe in the woods. I saw a prime example of the danger of gun-ignorant people handling rifles a few years later in Air Force basic training. My flight, along with several hundred other young men, were taken to the firing range to learn to shoot M-16s and hopefully to qualify for our marksmanship ribbons.

The big sergeant giving instructions was very clear on all points as he told us about the M-16 each time a new row of guys took their place on the firing line with gun in hand. But one point he must have repeated a dozen times, "Make sure you don't set your gun in automatic mode. Check it each time you begin a new series of shots."

Well, right next to me was a kid from New York City who had never had a real gun in his hands. Besides that, I don't think he was too bright. The first position we shot from was the sitting position. Sure enough, he shoved his gun into automatic mode and when the range commander gave the command, "Fire at will!" this guy pulled the trigger.

A funny thing happens to you the first time you shoot an automatic weapon, like a machine gun. It's even more pronounced if you're not expecting it. When you pull the trigger, the gun fairly comes alive as it tries to empty the entire magazine. With the gun jumping so rapidly, you just can't seem to get your finger off the trigger. In addition, the barrel starts climbing. It will continue to go up until you stop shooting or until you exert considerable force on it to keep it down. If you don't do anything, the barrel comes up over the top, and if there are enough bullets in the magazine, you end up leaning so far backward that you are shooting behind where you were originally aiming.

Well the kid from New York City didn't do anything, so his barrel was climbing fast. I prayed it wouldn't go vertical (I was thinking about all those arrows Colby shot straight up, scaring me to death). Quickly I shifted to praying the barrel didn't come over the top because, behind the greenhorn were about 250 other young guys waiting their turn. It could get really ugly—really deadly!

Just as the barrel was nearing the vertical position in its climb, a big combat boot came out of nowhere and stomped that barrel into the ground, forcing it back toward the targets. The M-16 continued its staccato belching until the clip was empty. That was when the big combat boot was removed by the big sergeant who replaced it with the largest string of four-letter words I've ever heard. That was followed by an impressive vocabulary of more intellectually oriented words designed to ridicule and, with surgical precision, thoroughly humiliate the young man.

I felt a little sorry for the ignorant city slicker, but that feeling was quickly replaced as I became thankful for the sergeant's big boot and quick reactions; because while I was earning my marksmanship ribbon by hitting 50 out of 50 silhouettes, the New York kid might have gotten his ribbon by shooting 50 real people. You don't wanna' get hit by a bullet from an M-16. There's a reason why a hit anywhere on the target silhouette is considered a kill. M-16 bullets tumble through the air and do horrible things to a human body. There is no such thing as being grazed by a bullet from an M-16!

Colby and I had graduated from Daisy's to Remingtons in our years of childhood friendship, but all good things, except God and heaven, must come to an end. I will never forget the last time Colby and I were together in the woods with our guns. We had a blast, but our guns didn't—we never even shot them. We had gone deer hunting behind the little white house one sunny warm October day. We ended up walking to the Chinamen's diggings, crossing them at the warm (west) fork of the Illinois River and continuing beyond for a few miles. It was growing late so we headed back toward Colby's house, but fearing we wouldn't make it before dark, we took a shortcut to save some walking. The drawback of this route was that we would have to cross the biggest Chinamen's diggings.

During the gold rush in Josephine County in the last half of the 19th century, Chinese immigrants were used to dig long, wide and deep trenches. The dirt extracted was run through sluice boxes to separate out the gold. Well, where we had to cross the diggings there was a U-shaped ditch 30 feet deep and about 60 feet across. The ditch had been dug through layers of red and yellow clay soil. The abundance of water caused the sides of the ditch to ooze moisture, creating ditch banks that were more slippery than either a greased pig or a water slide in a water park—take your pick.

As we walked toward the gaping ditch, guns in hand, Colby said, "I think we can just walk down here and up the other side—it looks like that's an animal trail."

"But the whole ditch is just wet clay—slicker than snot," I added as I looked at the thin sheet of shiny moisture glazing the clay on Colby's animal trail. I wasn't convinced that just because a deer walked that trail that we could also.

"I can get down here and up the other side. Just wait here, if you want to, 'til I cross."

Colby, gun in hand, took his first step down his animal trail at the top of the 30-foot deep ditch. His foot slipped so he brought the other foot alongside quickly to steady himself. That never happened. Both feet flew up into the air, Colby's gun fell on the ditch bank, barrel down, and started sliding with amazing speed toward the bottom of the ditch. When Colby came down on his rear and the small of his back, he yelled in surprise then started sliding down the bank at an amazing speed also. With his feet and hands up in the air he looked like he was making a scene for some old Laurel and Hardy movie. His gun reached the bottom before Colby and the barrel buried about 18 inches deep into the mud, packing its barrel with a mixture of red and yellow clay. Colby out-slid the gun, because he did not bury in at the bottom. Rather, he slid part way up the other side of the ditch then settled back into the bottom.

I stood at the top of the ditch laughing uncontrollably and finally managed to get out between guffaws, "Slapstick comedy doesn't get any better than that! And, look at your gun all clogged with clay—you won't be doing any more hunting today. And look at the red-clay stain in your jeans. Your Mom will never get that out! "

"I like to see you do any better!" Colby retorted, then added a complaint, "That stuff's impossible to walk on. It's slicker than that iced-over pond we tried to play motorcycle hockey on!"— that's definitely another story for another time.

Well I knew that clay was gonna be slick, but I was sure I could make it down unscathed.

"You just have to be more careful," I said stepping on to the clay successfully.

As I took my second step though, I repeated Colby's, scene gun barrel for gun barrel, slide for slide, stained jeans for stained jeans.

After I stopped in the bottom of the ditch, I looked up at Colby and shrugged. I then said what was on my mind and what I surmised was on Colby's mind ever since he slipped into the bottom of the ditch, "Both of our guns are plugged so deer hunting is over for today. You can't find a slide this fun except maybe in an amusement park. But this one's free—beat you to the top!"

We slid down both sides of the ditch for nearly an hour— sometimes starting from the top, sometimes starting from wherever we fell trying to climb to the top.

As the sun dipped toward the horizon drawing the day to a close, Colby's and my time hunting together had reached its sunset also. With clothes covered and irremediably stained with red clay, we started walking toward home.

After all was said and done, and despite the fact that boys will be boys, we hadn't shot anyone; we hadn't been shot; we had paid a price for occasionally violating gun safety rules, but we learned a lot during those years when Colby and I grew from Daisies to Remingtons.

Epilogue

Though at times I wouldn't have bet a plug nickel on it, Colby and I survived our childhood—God is merciful. Colby caused his parents a lot of worry due to his cleverness, imagination, and what I'll euphemistically call his daring. But he had a son who is now missing a finger or two—a son who paid Colby back in full for the worry—God is just.

Finally, in our late teens, Colby and I, at different times, both committed our lives to Christ—God is patient and very, very gracious. We had been raised in devout, church-going families but both delayed our decisions until adulthood stared us right in the face. I don't think either of us wanted to go there without Him in our lives and our lives in Him.

Colby went on to serve in the Navy on a nuclear sub (his Dad was on subs in WWII). I served in the Air Force as an intelligence analyst and then as a weather officer. Colby was able to get a leave from the Navy to be my best man when Babe and I got married. The Air Force did not reciprocate when Colby got married, so he and his new bride visited Babe and me, on their honeymoon, while I was in technical training in San Angelo, Texas.

After a couple of hitches in the Navy, Colby worked on computer systems for a large utility company in New Mexico.

After seven years in the Air Force, I went on to work as a research scientist at a national lab in the Pacific Northwest and recently retired after a second career developing computer systems for Boeing in Seattle.

Colby and I still keep in touch. But, as for adventures, we just reminisce—we have much more to reminisce about than one book could ever contain—also more than we dare put into a book.

Purposely I have not mentioned earlier that Colby and I both had baby brothers who came along just over seven years after us. Tim and Mike also became good friends and created their share of mischief—like the time they convinced my naïve Mom to cultivate a beautiful, healthy patch of marijuana in her flower bed. If they hadn't eventually told her the truth, she might still be watering, fertilizing and waiting for her little stash to produce those beautiful blooms she was told were coming from her "exotic plants."

Colby's brother, Tim, died very unexpectedly when he was still a young father—he is greatly missed. If their story is to be told, I'll leave that to my brother, Mike, or someone in Tim's family.

As for you, if I was a gambling man, I'd put money down that you people reading these stories also had good friends while growing up. Consequently you probably had your share of adventures. So, if you enjoyed my reflections on my childhood, I would encourage you to share your stories with the generations following you.

If you are so inclined, and I hope you are, here's all you have to do; just grab a notebook, a pencil with a good eraser, and start writing down the incidents that you remember. That's exactly what I did. I didn't stop until, nearly three months and twenty-two pencil-leads later, I had relived and re-enjoyed nearly 300 pages of Colby and Me.